My Doll My Style

SEWING FUN FASHIONS FOR YOUR 18-INCH DOLL

Anna Allen

the Quilting company

dedication

This book is dedicated to my husband, John, and my children, Carvel, Emma, Samuel, and Lucy. They are my steady rock and have been with me daily through this creative journey. Thank you for being my biggest support and inspiration.

fw

www.fwcommunity.com

22 21 20 19 18 5 4 3 2 1

SRN: R5955

ISBN-13: 978-1-4402-4826-9

Editorial Director
KERRY BOGERT

Editor
JODI BUTLER

Technical Editor
DEBRA FEHR GREENWAY

Art Director
ASHLEE WADSEN

Cover and Interior Designer
KARLA BAKER

Illustrator
MISSY SHEPLER

Photographer
ANNA ALLEN

Contents

Introduction

Hello and welcome!

Today's modern clothing styles are an exciting mix of color, texture, and materials. From lace to pleather, we see countless designs that allow us to communicate our personal style, whether classic or trendy. Shrinking these fashion trends down to doll-size scale is at the heart of this book. I've woven modern aesthetic and fit into projects that feature fantastic fashion fabrics. If these fabrics are new to you, there's no need to feel intimidated. I'm here for you! *My Doll, My Style* will show you how to sew with different types of fabric and feel empowered to sew beautiful doll clothes using fashionable fabrics. For tips, check out the Fabric Notes section that's included with each pattern. It is key to a successful project because I give specific suggestions to help you pick out fabulous fabric for each project.

I also included opportunities to add fashionable details to all the projects. The patterns include suggestions for different fabric choices, options to add trim, and appliqué placement ideas. There are even a few pattern variations for different sleeve and pant finishes. You can use these different fashion elements to create your own truly unique doll fashions!

I would love to see what you create, so please share your fun doll fashion creations online. Let's create beautiful doll fashions together, it's where the joy to create and the joy of play cross paths! #MyDollMyStyle.

happy sewing!
-Anna

CHAPTER ONE

Sewing Small Fashion

THERE ARE THREE KEY COMPONENTS to creating beautiful, fashionable, and easy-to-sew doll clothes. First, it's all about the fabric when sewing fashion. The Fabric Notes section in this chapter and accompanying sidebars throughout the book are packed with practical tips that will help you pick fabulous fabric for each project. Second is accurate cutting. You'll love the quick and precise methods in the Cutting Accurately section in this chapter. Third is sewing techniques.

In this chapter, you'll find tips for sewing knit and sequin fabrics. Sometimes people avoid sewing with these fabrics because they are too intimidated. I demystify sewing with these fabrics, and you will be delighted and empowered by the beautiful doll clothes you can make yourself!

The chapter also includes basic finishing techniques for the projects in this book, including instructions for hems, adding a knit waistband, and sewing a Velcro closure. Each pattern will refer back to the Finishing Techniques section when applicable, and there you will find the specific tips and directions you need.

Getting Started

TOOLS AND SUPPLIES

Here you will find the best tools for cutting out patterns quickly and accurately (see Cutting Accurately in this chapter for detailed directions), as well as the basic supplies and materials to complete the projects in this book. Take a look through the lists before starting a project to gather everything you will need for sewing and transferring pattern markings.

28 mm rotary cutter (21)

18 mm rotary cutter (22)

¼" (6 mm) soft stretch elastic

½" (1.3 cm) and ⅝" (1.5 cm) fold-over elastic

Anti-fray seam sealant

Bobbins (3)

Clear rotary cutting ruler

Clear tape (for taping pattern pieces together and to create fringe) (2)

Disappearing-ink fabric marker (14)

Double-sided wash-away transparent tape, such as wonder tape

Freezer paper (optional for cutting out templates)

Glue

Hand-sewing needles (9)

Iron and ironing board

Large safety pin (10) and or large needles (9)

Low-temperature heat gun and glue sticks

Measuring tape (1)

Paper-backed fusible web (such as Heat'N Bond Lite)

Pattern weights (washers) (1)

Pins and pincushion (6)

Pinking shears (20)

Point turner (23)

Printer paper

Scissors for fabric (19)

Scissors for paper

Seam gauge (ruler to measure hems) (12)

Seam ripper (8)

Self-healing cutting mat (18)

Sew On Soft & Flexible Velcro

Sew On Snag-Free Velcro (for lace)

Sewing machine needles: Ballpoint/jersey, stretch, all-purpose, denim, double, and Microtex (Sharp) needle for sewing faux leather (5)

Thimble (7)

Thread (4)

Tracing paper (15)

Tracing wheel (16)

Walking foot for your sewing machine (11)

Washers and weights (17)

Water-soluble marking pencil (13)

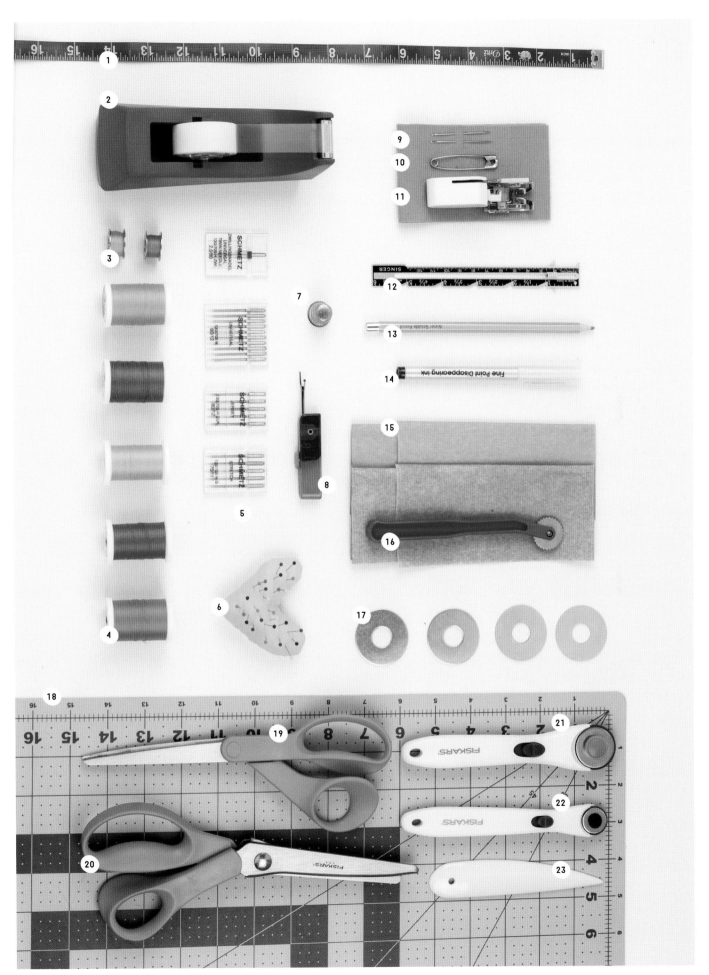

FASHION FIT

Fit is an important part of fashion, so I draft patterns with care to get a great fit. Let's go over a few details for how to get the best fit for your doll clothes.

The patterns and accessories in this book are designed for 18" (45.5 cm) play dolls. Because 18" (45.5 cm) dolls are made by a variety of companies, their body measurements and construction can vary by brand. Some dolls have fabric torsos, for example, while others are all vinyl. I fit the patterns in this book for a doll with a fabric torso. But even measurements for dolls with fabric torsos from the same company can vary because they are stuffed slightly differently. For your convenience, I've included a range of doll measurements so you can compare them with your particular 18" (45.5 cm) doll to get an idea of fit. Many of these patterns are sewn with knit fabric, which will be more flexible and forgiving with differences in size. For an 18" (45.5 cm) doll with a slim waist, you can make general adjustments by sewing the side seams with a larger seam allowance.

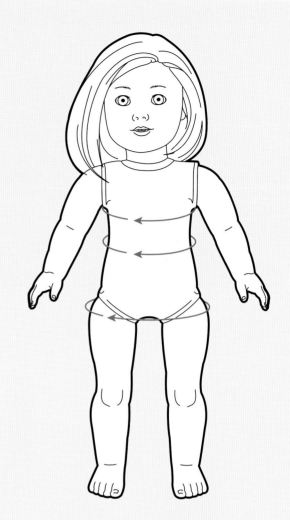

Doll measurements

CHEST (UNDER THE ARMS)
10¾–11" (27.5–28 cm)

WAIST
10¼–11" (26–28 cm)

HIP (WIDEST POINT AROUND THE BOTTOM AND HIPS)
12–12¼" (30.5–31 cm)

Fabric Notes

Woven Fabric Diagram

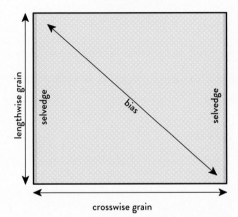

CHOOSING FABRIC

This section will help you confidently pick fabric for each project. Fabric has different properties and features. I keep this in mind when designing patterns and count on fabric to behave a certain way for a good fit. For each pattern in this book, I include suggestions for the type of fabric to use—either woven or knit—and the suggested weight. Patterns designed for knit fabrics also touch on stretch direction (the direction the fabric stretches) and stretch amount (how much a fabric will stretch). Before buying fabric, feel the weight and stretch qualities. This hands-on approach will give you the information you need to help you choose a great fabric for the project.

Fabric Type

Is your fabric a woven or a knit? Here are some general characteristics to keep in mind.

Wovens: Stretch on the bias with no horizontal or vertical stretch; edges fray.

Knits: Have either horizontal stretch or both horizontal and vertical stretch with low to no-fray edges.

Knit Fabric Diagram

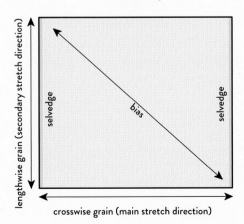

Fabric Weight

The weight or thickness of the fabric can range from a lightweight lace to a medium-weight knit or a heavyweight denim.

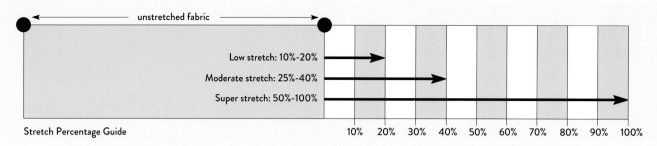

Stretch Percentage Guide

Pulling one side of your fabric across the stretch guide will show if it has low, moderate, or super stretch.

Note: The guide above is not to scale. To download the full-size Stretch Percentage Guide and the pattern pieces for this book, go to quiltingcompany.com/MyDollMyStyleTemplates.

STRETCH DIRECTION

For this book, stretch direction refers to the direction knit fabric stretches. Knowing the stretch direction will help you line up the pattern on the fabric correctly. Knit fabrics can sometimes seem to stretch every which way. To orient yourself to the fabric and its properties, it helps to figure out the main stretch direction as well as the secondary stretch direction.

Main Stretch Direction

The main stretch direction is the direction in which the fabric has the most stretch. It is typically perpendicular to the selvedge (also referred to as stretching across the grain). This is the stretch direction marked on the pattern pieces indicating how to orient the pattern piece with the fabric. See the Knit Fabric Diagram on the Fabric Notes page for reference.

Secondary Stretch Direction

The secondary stretch is parallel to the selvedge and also referred to as stretching with the grain. A knit may or may not have a secondary stretch.

2-Way Stretch or 4-Way Stretch

A combination of the main stretch direction and the secondary stretch direction is referred to as a 2-way stretch or a 4-way stretch.

2-Way Stretch

Main: Stretches perpendicular to the selvedge.

Secondary: Has very little to no stretch parallel to the selvedge.

4-Way Stretch

Main: Stretches perpendicular to the selvedge.

Secondary: Stretches parallel to the selvedge in a similar amount to the main stretch direction.

STRETCH AMOUNT

Another aspect of knit fabric is how much it stretches. This is often referred to as the stretch percentage. To simplify, I will divide stretch into three categories: low, moderate, and super. Each knit project in this book calls for a minimum stretch. For example, if a pattern calls for low stretch percentage, then that pattern can be sewn in a range of fabrics from a minimum, low-stretch knit to the highest super-stretch knit.

Low stretch: 10–20%

Moderate stretch: 25–40%

Super stretch: 50–100%

Determining Stretch

Use the stretch guide in the downloadable PDF to determine a fabric's stretch category (find it here: www.quiltingcompany.com/MyDollMyStyleTemplates). To do so:

1 First, measure the main stretch direction. Fold a 10" (25.5 cm) portion of fabric along the main stretch direction.

2 Line up the fabric with the dots on the stretch guide, then pinch the fold between your thumb and fingers at each dot.

3 Hold the fabric steady at the left dot, then stretch the fabric to the right beyond the second dot until you feel a firm resistance. This is the point on the guide that will indicate what stretch percentage or stretch category the knit fabric has.

4 Measure the secondary stretch direction. Refold a 10" (25.5 cm) portion of fabric in half along the secondary stretch direction.

5 Repeat steps 2 and 3 to determine the stretch percentage or stretch category for the secondary stretch direction.

Note: If a fabric stretches to an area between categories, then it is in the preceding category. For example, if the fabric stretches just short of the super-stretch section, that fabric is considered moderate stretch.

Stretch Recovery

It is important to choose fabric with good stretch recovery. Stretch recovery refers to a knit fabric's ability to return to the original shape after it is stretched. Poor stretch recovery leaves fabric distorted with stretched-out seams and misshapen projects. With good stretch recovery, fabric returns to the shape or close to the same shape it was in before you stretched it.

Cutting Accurately

Doll clothes are small, so accurately cutting the patterns out of fabric is important for a good fit. With that in mind, here are two methods for cutting out doll clothes patterns. Both begin with ironing the fabric so you start with a nice smooth surface.

ROTARY-CUTTER METHOD

This method for cutting out pattern pieces is quick and easy! You will need a rotary cutter and a self-healing mat. Start with the 28 mm rotary cutter. (The 18 mm rotary cutter is great for tight curves and turns.) For safety, rotary cutters are not recommended for kids.

MATERIALS

Fabric for your project

28 mm rotary cutter

18 mm rotary cutter (optional)

Self-healing mat

Pattern weights (you can also use washers or nickels)

Pattern printed on paper and cut out

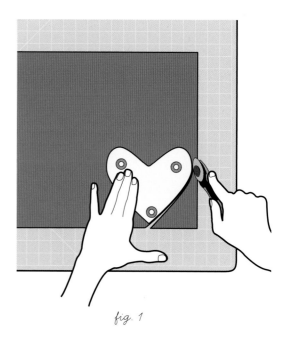

fig. 1

1   Lay out your fabric in a single layer or folded, if needed, on a self-healing mat.

2   Position the pattern piece on the fabric, then set pattern weights in the corners of the pattern and across the middle to hold it in place.

3   Hold the pattern with one hand, while cutting around the pattern with a rotary cutter (**Figure 1**).

SCISSORS AND FREEZER-PAPER METHOD

For this method, print the pattern pieces onto freezer paper, then cut them out and temporarily adhere them to the fabric with a hot iron. It is easiest to work with a single layer of fabric, so print off multiple pattern pieces when the pattern says "cut 2."

Note: This method will only work on fabric that can be ironed on high heat. Test your fabric first.

MATERIALS

Freezer paper

Clear tape

Fabric scissors and paper-cutting scissors

Iron and ironing board

Pattern printed onto paper (uncut)

Fabric for your project

1   Cut freezer paper down to size so that it will cover the patterns that are printed on the sheets of paper. Tape the freezer paper, shiny side down, over the printed copy of the pattern. Run the paper through your printer, printing the pattern onto the freezer paper.

2   Remove the tape and cut out the pattern pieces.

3   On an ironing board, arrange the freezer-paper patterns, shiny side down, on the fabric. Using a high setting, iron the freezer-paper pattern pieces to the fabric for 10–15 seconds per section. Let the fabric and freezer paper cool, then test a corner of the freezer paper to make sure the pattern adhered (**Figure 2**).

4   Cut out fabric pattern pieces, then peel off freezer paper (**Figure 3**).

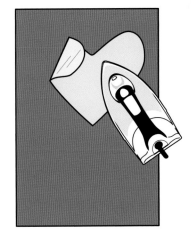

fig. 2

fig. 3

Transferring Pattern Markings

Use these directions to transfer pattern markings, including notches, dots, and stitch lines, to cut out fabric easily and accurately. A disappearing-ink fabric marker is my go-to for marking because it is gentle on knits and specialty fabrics. A light-colored water-soluble marking pencil is an option for dark fabrics. The marks from tracing paper, marking pencils, and disappearing-ink fabric markers come off easily with just a little water. For specialty fabric that is hard to mark, use a pin in the fabric at each dot or notch.

TAKE CARE WHEN ARRANGING PATTERN PIECES THAT ARE CUT ON FOLDED FABRIC, SO THE ORIENTATION IS CORRECT.

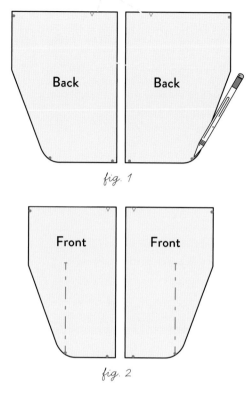

fig. 1

fig. 2

MATERIALS

Pins

Scissors

Disappearing-ink fabric marker

Tracing wheel

Tracing paper

Water-soluble marking pencil (optional)

DOTS

Place a finger on the dot on the paper pattern. (Your finger will provide counterpressure while you mark the dot.) For a single layer of fabric, lift up the edge of the paper and place the disappearing-ink fabric marker between the paper pattern and the fabric. For a double layer of fabric, place the marker between the layers of fabric. Mark a dot with the tip of the marker **(Figure 1)**.

NOTCHES

After the pattern piece is cut out of fabric, leave the pattern weights on the paper pattern to mark the notches. Place a finger on the paper pattern at the point of the notch. Lift up the edge of the paper just enough so the fabric marker can fit between the paper pattern and the fabric, then mark ¼" (6 mm) line (shown as a triangle in the illustrations above) from the notch point toward the edge of the fabric (refer to **Figure 1** and **Figure 2**).

STITCH LINES

For best results, follow the instructions for your tracing paper. To transfer a specific stitch line, place the tracing paper between the paper pattern and a single layer of fabric with the colored side facing the fabric. Trace the stitch line on to the pattern with a tracing wheel **(Figure 2)**.

Sewing with Knits and Sequin Fabrics

SEWING WITH KNITS

Use these tips to make sewing with knit fabrics easier and get better results.

× Take a test run. A simple stitch test on a knit fabric can help you understand how the fabric will behave and give you clues about any adjustments that you may need to make to have success.

× Use a ballpoint/jersey needle (see Tools and Supplies). The shape of the tip lets it pass through the loops in knit fabrics without breaking the fibers. It will also help with skipped stitches, a common struggle when sewing knits.

× If a project calls for a double needle, test it on a scrap of fabric first. You may need to increase the thread tension a bit (this is common). If you are using the double needle to finish a hem, check the distance the stitches are from the edge. Go slowly. It can help you get a better finish. Use the bobbin for the second matching thread and a different bobbin for the under thread. (For more tips, see Sewing Hems.)

× To prevent fabric from being pushed into the needle plate, hold the tail threads when you start stitching. Pull the threads as you stitch.

× Lengthen stitches. This small adjustment can make a big difference when stitching with knits.

× Topstitch with a long, narrow zigzag stitch in areas that need minimal stretch. This stitch is more subtle than a regular zigzag stitch. (Unless your project needs a lot of stretch.)

× Use a regular zigzag stitch on the inside of the project where it needs the most stretch.

× Press fabric. Following the heat settings for your chosen fabric, press the seam lines to flatten and shrink down the area. This can make a huge difference in how a seam sits.

× Unfinished edges are a quick way to finish a project and give it a trendy look. Before leaving a hem unfinished, test how much the cut edge of the fabric curls. Minimal curl is recommended for leaving the edges unfinished on projects. The knit should also be no-fray on the edges.

× Try a walking foot on your sewing machine. It helps move fabric through your machine evenly and smoothly and makes a huge difference with minimal investment. Take note, it is not a ¼" (6 mm) foot, so you will need to check to make sure you are sewing with the correct seam allowances. Don't use a walking foot when sewing with a double needle as it may cause your needle to break.

SEWING SEQUIN FABRIC

There are a variety of sequin fabrics. For the projects in this book, I recommend using sequin fabric on a knit or netting fabric backing with sequins that are sewn on the fabric, not glued. The sequins are attached to the fabric with the thread that passes through the hole one to three times. They can be multiple sizes and shapes.

Cutting Sequin Fabric

To reduce bulk, follow these steps to remove sequins from the seam allowance before you start sewing.

MATERIALS

Sequin fabric

Rotary cutter

Scissors

Ruler

1   Place the pattern pieces on the wrong side of the fabric. Cut out the pattern on the line with a rotary cutter.

2   Measure the seam allowance. To remove several sequins at a time, pinch a row of sequins. Cut the sequins in half without cutting through the thread that connects them. (The sequins are stitched on with a continuous string, so if you cut the thread more sequins will come off.)

3   Repeat steps 1 and 2 to remove sequins on every side that will be in the seam allowance.

4   When you're done stitching the project you can hand-sew some of the sequins back on where the pattern is interrupted.

Tips for Sewing Sequins

• On regular seams, don't sew through the sequins. On hems, after removing sequins from the seam allowance, you can stitch over the sequins on the right side of the fabric.

• Go slowly. It will help you achieve a better finish.

• Use a heavier gauge needle. Sewing through sequins dulls the needle, so you will need to change it more often.

• Top stitch a seam allowance where needed to help it lie flatter.

• Use a walking foot to help the sequins move through the machine more smoothly and not stick. Hold the tail threads when you start stitching. This will help bulky fabric not get pushed down in the plate and get stuck.

TIPS FOR ADDING TRIM

There are some projects that have an option for adding trim, including ¼" (6 mm) and ½" (1.3 cm) pom-pom trim, and ½" (1.3 cm) and 2" (5 cm) lace. The following tips will help simplify the process.

- When adding trim to knit fabric, be careful not to stretch the fabric while pinning or stitching the trim (**Figure 1**). Stretching the fabric can result in distorted or misshapen hemlines.

- Wonder tape is an excellent alternative to pinning on trim. It's quicker and easier to manage the small pieces. For long pieces of trim, cut sections of wonder tape and finger press it in place. Peel off the backing and adhere to the second surface.

- For most projects, use both a regular zigzag stitch and a straight stitch to securely sew on trim. Using both stitches is helpful with the small seam allowances.

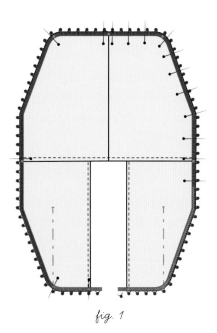

fig. 1

Finishing Techniques

SEWING HEMS

You can choose from three different hems for the projects in this book. The Single-Fold Hem with a Double Needle and the Single-Fold Hem with a Zigzag Stitch are interchangeable. They each have a different look but create tidy hems. The Double-Fold Hem is used for sturdy edges and has a clean finish that encases the fraying edges of woven fabrics.

DON'T USE A WALKING FOOT WHEN SEWING WITH A DOUBLE NEEDLE. IT MAY CAUSE YOUR NEEDLE TO BREAK.

Single-Fold Hem with a Double Needle

Use this technique to finish necklines, sleeves, and hemlines. The double needle creates a professional-looking finish, and the stretchy stitch is perfect for knits. Before you begin, test the double needle on a scrap of fabric. Set the sewing machine to a regular straight stitch. The stitches should be even and consistent with no skips and a zigzag stitch pattern on the wrong side of the fabric. If your stitches do not follow this pattern, you may need to increase the tension a bit (this is common). Depending on the weight and stretch of the knit, some knits are more prone to being pushed down by the needle into the needle plate. If this happens, start sewing ¼–½" (6 mm–1.3 cm) from the starting point and hold the tail threads when you start stitching. Pull the threads as you stitch. Instead of using two spools of thread, use the matching bobbin for the second thread, then choose a different bobbin for the back-side thread. Go slowly for more control and a better finish. Press the seam for a great finish.

1 Referring to **Figure 1**, fold and pin the edges as follows. For straight and curved edges, fold and pin each end and the center ¼" (6 mm) to the wrong side. For necklines, fold and pin the edge ¼" (6 mm) to the wrong side at the shoulder seams, center front, and center back.

2 Continue folding and pinning the edge with pins placed ½–1" apart (1.3–2.5 cm) (**Figure 2**).

3 On the right side of the fabric, stitch a scant ¼" (6 mm) from the fold with a double needle and press (**Figure 3**).

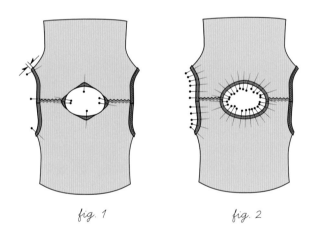

fig. 1   *fig. 2*

fig. 3

Single-Fold Hem with a Zigzag Stitch

Here's another single-fold hem for necklines, sleeves, and hemlines. Use the regular zigzag stitch when you need the seam to stretch. And use the long, narrow zigzag stitch when you don't need maximum stretch (it has a more professional-looking finish than the regular zigzag stitch). Test this stretchy stitch out on your knit fabric first. When you pull the seam line, the stitches should stretch with the fabric. If the stitches break, then you need to adjust to a wider zigzag stitch.

1   Repeat the same technique to fold and pin the edges from steps 1 and 2 in the Single-Fold Hem with a Double Needle directions.

2   On the right side of the fabric, stitch a scant ¼" (6 mm) from the fold with a long, narrow zigzag stitch and press (**Figure 4**).

Double-Fold Hem

The double-fold hem offers a neat and tidy finish. It works well on light- to medium-weight wovens and hides the fray on cut edges. There are a couple of knit patterns that call for it, too. Refer to **Figure 5** for steps 1–3.

1   Fold the fabric edge ¼" (6 mm) to the wrong side.

2   Fold another ¼" (6 mm) to the wrong side to create a double-fold hem.

3   Pin along the fold, then stitch on the right side with a seam allowance that is less than ¼" (6 mm) to catch the folded fabric in the seam. Press.

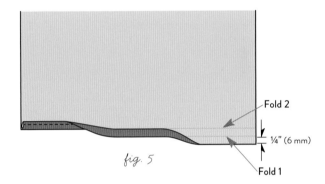

Fold 2
¼" (6 mm)
Fold 1

fig. 5

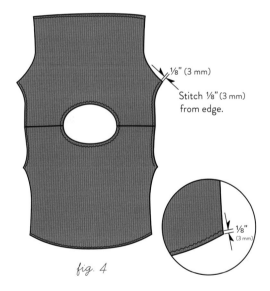

⅛" (3 mm)
Stitch ⅛" (3 mm) from edge.

⅛" (3 mm)

fig. 4

ADDING A KNIT WAISTBAND

Several projects in this book have a knit waistband. Follow the specific project directions, referring to these instructions when adding the waistband.

MATERIALS

Lightweight knit, ⅛ yard (11.5 cm)

⅝" (1.5 cm) fold-over elastic, 10½" (26.5 cm) length

Thread: Coordinating with main fabric and waistband; contrasting thread for topstitching (optional)

Pencil or disappearing-ink fabric marker

Waistband pattern pieces: Waistband, Waistband Marking Guide

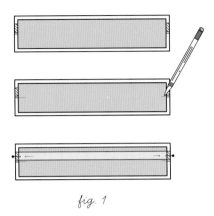

fig. 1

1   Place the waistband piece on the marking guide and mark the center on each side. Match the elastic ends with the corresponding lines on the guide and pin on each end (**Figure 1**).

2   Fold the waistband in half lengthwise, lining up the center markings and elastic ends. Pin along the edge, then straight stitch the end (**Figure 2**).
    Note: This seam line is the center back of the waistband.

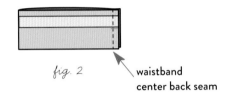

fig. 2 — waistband center back seam

3   Refer to **Figure 3**. With the waistband wrong-side out, fold up the center back seam and pin in place. Continue folding the fabric over the elastic, making sure the elastic stays next to the fold. Fold the waistband in half lengthwise with the center back seam on one side and place a pin to mark the fold on each end. Refold the waistband with the two pins in the center, then place a pin to mark the fold on each end.

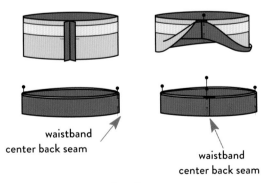

waistband center back seam

waistband center back seam

fig. 3

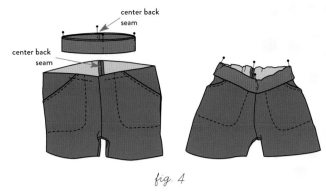

fig. 4

4 With the garment front side up, arrange the waistband over the pants or shorts, lining up the cut edges of the waistband and the garment as well as the center back seams. Match the three other pins on the waistband with the side seams (on the shorts, match with the dots) and front center seam on the pants or shorts. Pin the waistband and pants together at these points (**Figure 4**).

5 To evenly distribute the waistband around the garment waistline, stretch the waistband between two pins and place a pin (**Figure 5**). Continue around the waistband, stretching the knit waistband between two pins and placing a pin, until the waistband is securely and evenly placed around the waistline (**Figure 6**).

6 Using a regular zigzag stitch, sew from pin to pin, stretching the knit waistband slightly to match up with the pants waistline (**Figure 7**) to attach the waistband (**Figure 8**).

7 Turn the waistband to the right side with the seam allowance facing down and press the seam.

8 On the right side of the project, pin along the waistline seam, pinning through the waistband on the front of the fabric seam allowance through the back side of the fabric (**Figure 9**).

9 Using a straight stitch for wovens and a long, narrow zigzag stitch for knits, topstitch on the garment side of the waistline. Stitch from pin to pin, slightly stretching the fabric flat as you go (**Figure 10**). Press the topstitching.

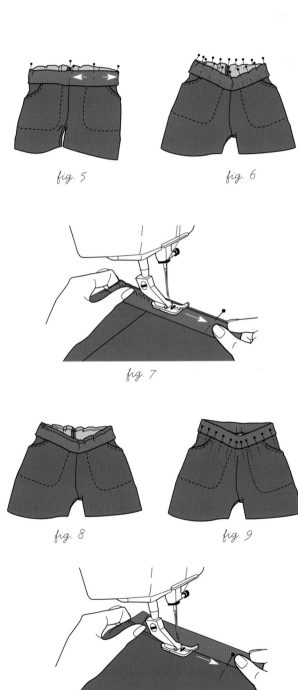

fig. 5   fig. 6

fig. 7

fig. 8   fig. 9

fig. 10

VELCRO CLOSURES

Velcro closures are used for several patterns in this book. Follow the specific pattern instructions, then refer to these directions when installing the Velcro.

Sew On Soft & Flexible Velcro is more flexible and has a nicer look for doll clothes, while Sew On Snag-Free Velcro is better for projects made with lace or netting fabric. Trim the Velcro to size and stitch slowly for better results. For easy Velcro placement, use pieces of wonder tape instead of pins.

Note: The hook side of Sew On Soft & Flexible Velcro is stiffer, while the loop side is soft so its fibers can catch in the hook side. For Sew On Snag-Free Velcro, the hook and loop sides are the same.

MATERIALS

Thread to coordinate with Velcro and main fabric

Universal sewing needle size 90/14 or 80/12 (thick needles stitch better on Velcro)

Sew On Soft & Flexible Velcro or Sew On Snag-Free Velcro

Pins or wonder tape

Scissors

Ruler

Pencil or disappearing-ink fabric marker

Velcro Closures for Tops

Follow these directions for the Lace Panel Top and Athletic Top.

1   Use a regular zigzag stitch right on the edge of the fabric (with no seam allowance) of the left and right back opening to stabilize the cut edge.

2   With the hook and loop sides connected, mark and trim a length of Velcro to ⅜" (1 cm) wide (length will vary by pattern).

3   On the right side of the fabric, pin the loop Velcro to the right back opening. Starting at the neckline edge, straight stitch each side of the Velcro along the length, close to the Velcro edge (**Figure 1**).

4   Pin the hook Velcro to the left back opening on the right side of the fabric. Starting from the neckline edge, straight stitch each side of the Velcro along the length, close to the Velcro edge (**Figure 2**).

5   Fold the Velcro on the left back ⅜" (1 cm) to the wrong side as shown and pin (**Figure 3**).

fig. 1

fig. 2

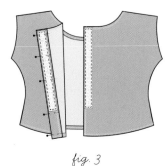

fig. 3

6 With the right side of the fabric facing up, topstitch the left back side from the neckline edge to the hem about ⅜" (1 cm) from the folded edge, catching the Velcro in the seam and press. Edgestitch down the left back opening, catching the Velcro in the seam (**Figure 4**). Press.

fig. 4

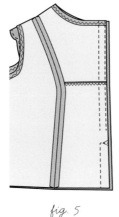

fig. 5

Velcro Closures for Tunics and Dresses

These instructions are for the Long Sleeve Tunic, Flutter Sleeve Dress, Flutter Sleeve Tunic, and the A-Line Dress.

1 Follow steps 1–4 for Velcro Closures for Tops.

2 Turn the garment wrong side out and close the Velcro closure. Match and pin the fabric below the Velcro from the notch to the bottom edge of the garment. Stitch from the fabric edge across the notch ⅜" (1 cm). Stitch from the notch to the bottom edge with ⅜" (1 cm) seam allowance (**Figure 5**).

3 Follow steps 5–6 for Velcro Closures for Tops to finish.

Note: Only topstitch and edgestitch the length of the Velcro on the left back (don't continue and sew to the bottom edge of the dress or tunic).

CHAPTER TWO

Doll Fashions

ENJOY SWEET STYLES for spring and summer and cozy layers for fall and winter. There's fashion and style to sew for every season, so you can create a beautiful and versatile wardrobe for your doll.

tips for success

Keep these tips in mind when sewing the patterns in this book.

- The templates for this book can be downloaded here: www.quiltingcompany.com/MyDollMyStyleTemplates

- Sew projects with ¼" (6 mm) seam allowance unless the instructions say otherwise.

- Trim the seam allowance with scissors or pinking shears very slightly, if at all, to reduce bulk in the seams.

- Joining pattern pieces: Some of the patterns are split into two sections that need to be joined together before you cut out the fabric. Line up the edges that have shapes to indicate where the patterns are to be joined. Tape the pattern pieces together on the front and back edges.

- Press fabric that is tolerant to heat with an iron before you start and between steps.

- Clip the curves to create smooth seams when you turn the garment right side out. When sewing small fashions, there are two ways to clip the curves. Option A: Clip the curve and trim the seam allowance with pinking shears. Option B: Make a little notch in the seam allowance on convex curves and clip slits in the seam allowance for concave curves.

Fringe Swimsuit

This swimsuit creates a splash with fun layered fringe along the front edge. The provided cutting guide helps you cut the fringe straight and even. The gently curved front neckline is sweet, and the edges of the suit are all finished with ¼" (6 mm) elastic.

MATERIALS

Swimsuit or performance knit for main fabric, ¼ yard (0.2 m)

Contrasting color swimsuit or performance knit for fringe (optional), ⅛ yard (11.5 cm)

Thread: Coordinating with main fabric

¼" (6 mm) wide soft stretch elastic, 24" (61 cm) length, cut into (2) 6" (15 cm) segments and (1) 12" (30.5 cm) segment

½–⅝" (1.3–1.5 cm) wide fold-over elastic, (2) 5" (12.5 cm) segments

Fringe Swimsuit pattern pieces: Front, Back, Fringe, and Fringe Cutting Guide

All seam allowances are ¼" (6 mm) unless otherwise noted.

FABRIC NOTES

Main and contrasting fabric: This pattern calls for fabric with a lot of stretch! Swimsuit knits are known for their 4-way super stretch and great stretch recovery. For the best fringe, use no-fray fabric. Use one or two colors for the fringe. Adding a solid color of fringe under a patterned fringe will make it stand out.

1   Using the pattern pieces, cut out the fabric. Transfer the notches and dots on the pattern to the fabric with a disappearing-ink fabric marker (see Transferring Pattern Markings in chapter 1 for details).

2   Make the fringe (see Fool-Proof Fringe for detailed directions).

3   Arrange the front and back pieces with right sides together, lining up the edges. Pin the side seams at the top and bottom, then pull the fabric on each side between the pins so it's even and place another pin. Stitch the seam with a regular zigzag stitch (**Figure 1**). Trim the seam allowance slightly.

4   Turn the suit right side out. Match the notches on the front and fringe pieces and pin in place. Match the sides of the fringe with the front side seams and pin, then pin across the upper edge (**Figure 2**).

5   Using a regular zigzag stitch and working from side seam to side seam, sew across the upper edge of the fringe and front with no seam allowance (**Figure 3**).

fig. 1

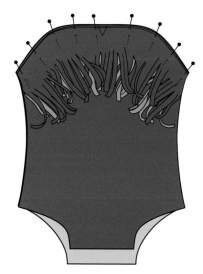

fig. 2

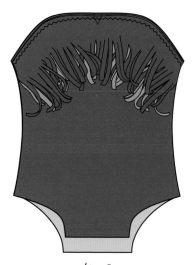

fig. 3

FOOL-PROOF FRINGE

MATERIALS

No-fray swimwear knit for fringe pieces

Scotch tape

28 mm rotary cutter

Self-healing mat

Rotary cutter ruler

Fool-Proof Fringe pattern piece: Fringe Cutting Guide

1   Tape the fringe-cutting guide to a self-healing mat along the top and sides.

2   Line up 1 fabric piece in the center of the box, then tape the fabric to the Fringe Cutting Guide along the narrow side of the tape line. Layer and tape the second fabric piece on top of the first in the same manner. If cutting fringe layers that are different lengths, layer the shortest layer on the Fringe Cutting Guide and the longest layer on the top.

3   Line up the ruler with the first line on the guide, matching the line above and below the fabric. Hold the ruler in place with one hand, then cut from the bottom of the fabric up to the tape line.

4   Move the ruler to the next line and cut. Continue cutting across the length of the fabric. Then remove the tape.

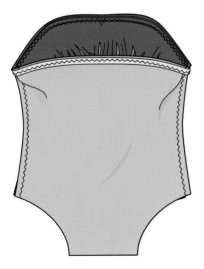

fig. 4

6   Turn the swimsuit wrong side out so the fringe is on the inside. Using the 12" (30.5 cm) length of ¼" (6 mm) elastic, overlap one end ¼" (6 mm) at the top of the side seam of the front and back (with no seam allowance). Starting at the side seam, stitch the elastic along the edge of the front and back, pulling the elastic with a little tension as you stitch and keeping the fringe out of the way. Overlap the starting point by ¼" (6 mm), then trim off the extra elastic (**Figure 4**).

7 Fold the 5" (12.5 cm) segments of fold-over elastic in half lengthwise with wrong sides together. Pin and stitch the open side of the elastic with a regular zigzag stitch.

8 With the swimsuit right side out, match the end of the fold-over elastic to the dot on the front and line up the fold-over elastic edge with the top edge of the swimsuit. Using a straight stitch, sew the end of the fold-over elastic in place ¼" (6 mm) from the swimsuit edge and backstitch to reinforce the stitching. Repeat with the other strap (**Figure 5**).

9 Fold down the edge of the front and back of the suit ¼" (6 mm) toward the wrong side. Pull the straps up away from the fabric. Pin the upper edge of the swimsuit along the top of the fringe, making sure the fabric is pinned snugly with the two layers of fringe smooth along the edge (**Figure 6**). Then pin along the back edge. Stitch a scant ¼" (6 mm) from the edge with a long, narrow zigzag stitch, stitching through the ¼" (6 mm) elastic.

10 Turn the swimsuit wrong side out with the front and back leg opening flat. Line up a 6" (15 cm) segment of ¼" (6 mm) elastic along the leg and overlap one end of the opening by ¼" (6 mm) (**Figure 7**). Stitch the

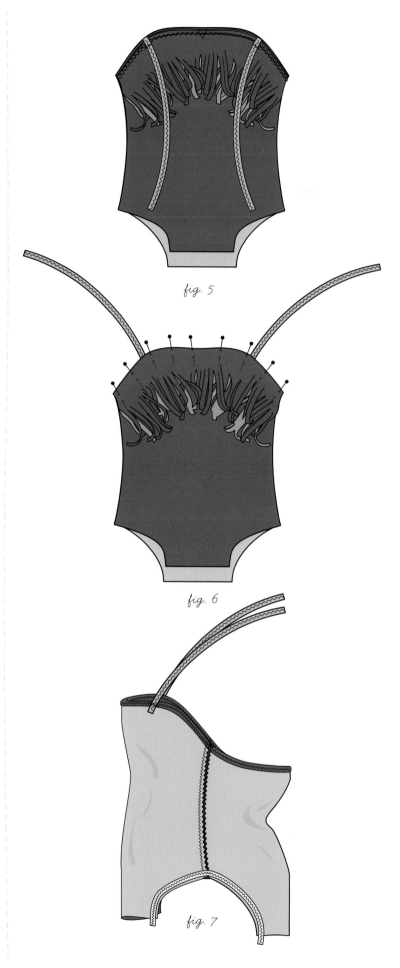

fig. 5

fig. 6

fig. 7

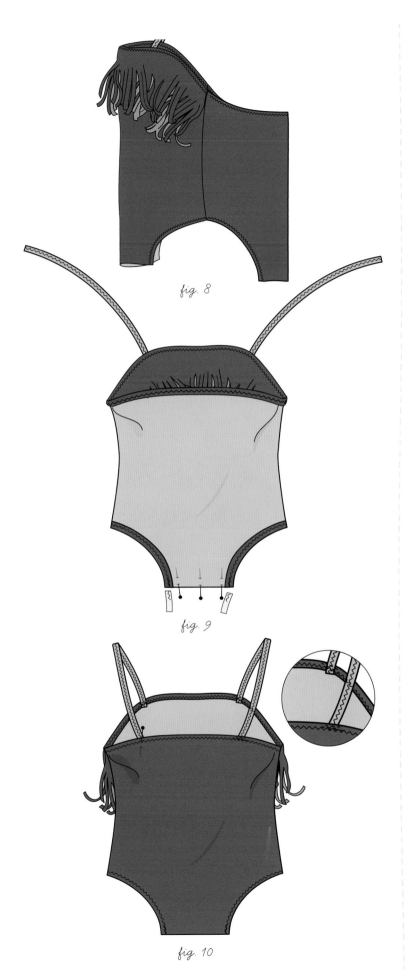

fig. 8

fig. 9

fig. 10

elastic along the edge of the leg opening with a regular zigzag stitch (with no seam allowance). To keep a maximum stretch on the leg opening, don't pull the elastic as you stitch. There will be extra elastic. Sew the other 6" (15 cm) segment of the ¼" (6 mm) elastic on the other leg opening.

11 Turn the swimsuit right side out. Fold the leg elastic toward the wrong side, smooth the fabric, and pin. Sew a scant ¼" (6 mm) from the edge with a long, narrow zigzag stitch, sewing through the elastic (**Figure 8**).

12 With right sides together, match up the front and back leg openings and pin. Stitch with a long, narrow zigzag stitch, then trim off extra elastic (**Figure 9**).

13 Turn the swimsuit right side out and put it on a doll. Pin the elastic ends on the back dots. Adjust the length of the straps to fit the doll and pin (the elastic is longer than you need). Be sure to position the straps so the front is smooth with no wrinkles under the fringe. Take the swimsuit off the doll. Using a straight stitch, sew the elastic ¼" (6 mm) from the back edge. Reinforce by stitching the elastic straps along the top edge of the back. Trim the straps, if needed (**Figure 10**).

Swimsuit cover-up

Sweet and summery, this cool cover-up pairs draping sleeves with pom-pom trim for a playful look that's just right for some fun in the sun.

MATERIALS

Light- to medium-weight knit, ¼ yard (0.2 m)

Thread: Coordinating with trim and fabric

¼" (6 mm) pom-pom trim, 49" (124.5 cm) strip

Swimsuit Cover-up pattern pieces: Front, Back

All seam allowances are ¼" (6 mm) unless otherwise noted.

FABRIC NOTES

Main fabric: For a light and airy look, use a lightweight knit with at least a 2-way stretch across the grain, moderate to super stretch, and a good drape, such as a knit T-shirt, a lace stretch knit, or an open-weave knit.

UPCYCLE TIP

This adorable accessory can be made from a repurposed T-shirt.

1 Using the pattern pieces, cut out the fabric. Mark the dots, notches, and side seam stitch lines on the front and back fabric pieces with a disappearing-ink fabric marker (see Transferring Pattern Markings in chapter 1 for tips).

2 Following the Double-Fold Hem directions in chapter 1, finish the long edge of the two front pieces (**Figure 1**).

3 With right sides together, match and pin the back pieces together along the straight edge. Sew along the edge with ¼" (6 mm) seam allowance (**Figure 2**). Press the seam open.

4 With right sides together, match the notches on the front and back pieces. Pin between the notches and the sleeve edges (**Figure 3**). Starting at one end, straight stitch from sleeve edge to sleeve edge to create the shoulder seam. With the wrong side out, press the shoulder seam allowance across the neckline toward the back.

5 On the right side, pin the seam allowance toward the back. With the right side out, topstitch the seam allowance to the back (**Figure 4**).

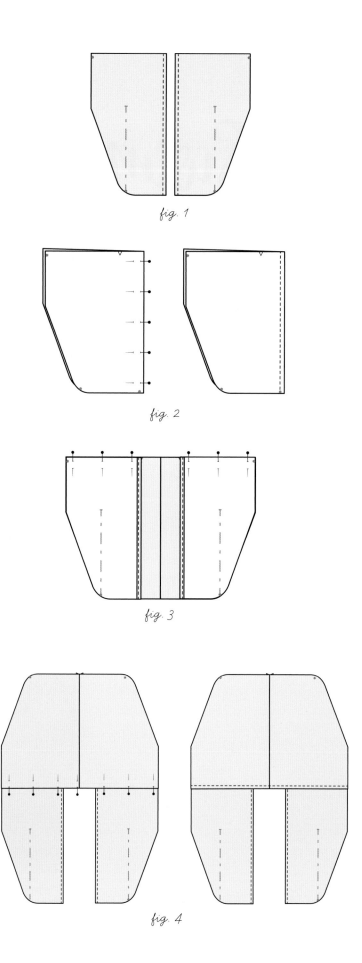

fig. 1

fig. 2

fig. 3

fig. 4

TRIM PLACEMENT TIPS

Trim can stretch with the fabric edge as you place it, which can cause the trim to not line up properly. If you want extra help lining up the trim and cover-up edges evenly, set the length of trim on a flat surface and tape down each end (do not stretch the trim). Starting on one end of the trim, and using a measuring tape, mark a dot at the measurements below using a disappearing-ink fabric marker.

Note: The measurements are for the trim and coordinate with the dots marked on the cover-up in step 1 (when helpful, the placement of the dot is noted after the measurement).

½" (1.3 cm) (front opening)

3" (7.5 cm) (side seam)

8¾" (22 cm)

11 ⅞" (30 cm) (shoulder seam)

15" (38 cm)

20¾" (52.5 cm)

24½" (62 cm) (center back)

28¼" (72 cm)

34" (86.5 cm)

37⅛" (94.5 cm) (shoulder seam)

40¼" (102 cm)

46" (117 cm) (side seam)

48½" (123 cm) (front opening)

The first dot marked at ½" (1.3 cm) and the last dot marked at 48½" (123 cm) are the starting and ending points for the trim placement and coordinate with the dots on the cover-up at the folded edges of the front opening. With right sides up, overlap the trim on the fabric around the perimeter of the cover-up matching and pinning the dots on the length of trim with the dots along the edge of the cover-up. Then follow the directions in step 6 to sew on the trim.

6 With the right side up, overlap the trim on the fabric around the perimeter of the cover-up with the trim overhanging each side by ½" (1.3 cm) and pin in place (see Trim Placement Tips for details). Using a regular zigzag stitch, sew through the trim and fabric with a matching thread (with no seam allowance). To finish the ends, cut off the pom-poms on the segment of trim that is beyond the edges of the front opening, then fold the extra trim to the wrong side of the fabric, pin, and stitch in place (**Figure 5**).

7 Fold the cover-up along the shoulder seam with the wrong sides together, lining up the front and back edges. Pin through both layers along the front side seam lines. In a matching thread, straight stitch from the top of the stitch line toward the fabric/trim edge to create the side seam and arm openings (**Figure 6**).

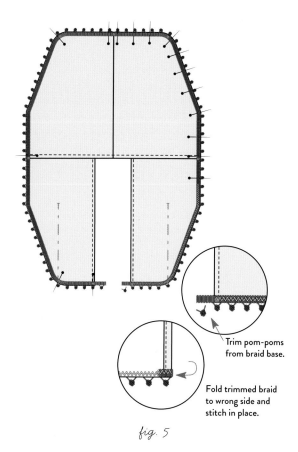

Trim pom-poms from braid base.

Fold trimmed braid to wrong side and stitch in place.

fig. 5

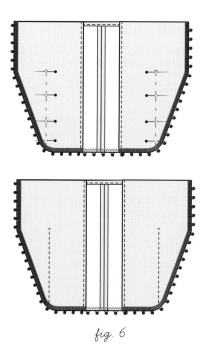

fig. 6

Swim sarong

This light and breezy sarong pairs perfectly with the Fringe Swimsuit. The simple tie in the front is both functional and adorable. For an extra-fun detail, add pom-pom trim to the edge of the Swim Sarong.

MATERIALS

Woven fabric for the sarong and tie, ¼ yard (0.2 m)

Thread: Coordinating with main fabric and trim

¼" (6 mm) pom-pom trim, 46" (117 cm) strip (optional)

Swim Sarong pattern pieces: Sarong Left, Sarong Right, Left Facing, Right Facing

All seam allowances are ¼" (6 mm) unless otherwise noted.

FABRIC NOTES

Main fabric: Lightweight cotton, such as quilting cotton and cotton shirting, has the right look and drape. For a quick and easy way to reduce fray, clip the curves and trim the seam allowance with pinking shears.

1   Arrange the sarong pattern pieces on the wrong side of the fabric and cut out. Arrange the facing pattern pieces on the right side of the fabric and cut out. Transfer the notches and dots on the patterns to the fabric with a disappearing-ink fabric marker (see Transferring Pattern Markings in chapter 1 for details).

2   Finish the bottom edge of the facing pieces with a regular zigzag stitch or trim with pinking shears to prevent fraying (with no seam allowance).

3   With right sides together, match the notches on the facing with the notches on the sarong. Pin along the top edge and around the ties, then straight stitch the edges where the facing and sarong match up (**Figure 1**).

4   Clip the curves and the corner under the ties (**Figure 2**). Turn right side out and press.

5   Sew around the unfinished edge on the sarong with a regular zigzag stitch and no seam allowance (**Figure 3**).

6   Fold the unfinished edge ¼" (6 mm) to the wrong side and pin. Sew around the edge with a straight stitch (**Figure 4**).

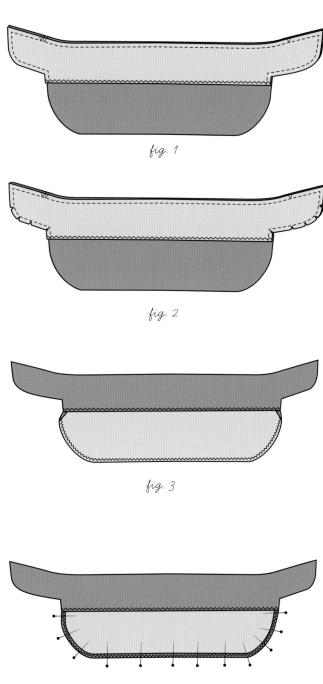

fig. 1

fig. 2

fig. 3

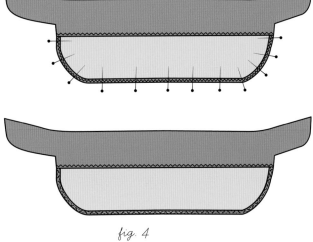

fig. 4

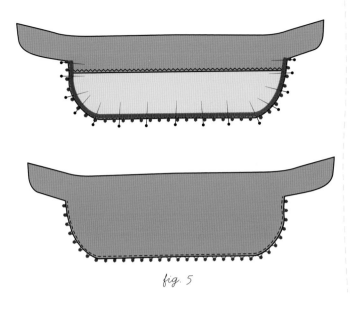

7   Add trim to the skirt (optional). Following the Tips for Adding Trim in chapter 1, sew the pom-pom trim to the wrong side of the sarong, starting at the edge of the tie and working across the sarong hem to end at the other tie (**Figure 5**).

fig. 5

Beach Bag

This cool tote features a flat bottom and a curved seam along the opening edge. The inside is finished with a contrasting lining to hide the seams. The flat front and back offer plenty of space to add your own embellishments, such as the three sewn-on pom-poms shown here.

MATERIALS

Denim or canvas for main fabric, ¼ yard (0.2 m)

Woven fabric for lining, ¼ yard (0.2 m)

Denim needle

Thread: Coordinating with main fabric and lining

Beach Bag pattern pieces: Front and Back (1 piece), Base, Handle; Small Pom-Pom template

Pom-poms (optional; see Making Pom-Poms following Beach Bag directions)

Low-temperature heat gun and glue sticks or hand-sewing needle and thread (for attaching the pom-poms; optional)

All seam allowances are ¼" (6 mm) unless otherwise noted.

FABRIC NOTES

Main fabric: Medium-weight fabric, such as denim or canvas, is a must to give this bag shape. You can repurpose a pair of jeans and center the yellow side seam stitching (as shown in the photo) or add decorative stitching to add fun details to the bag.

Lining fabric: Choose a lightweight woven, such as quilting cotton, with a fun print.

UPCYCLE TIP

This bag can be made from a pair of old jeans (see Fabric Notes for details).

1   Using the pattern pieces,
cut out the fabric. Transfer
the notches and dots on the
pattern to the fabric with a
disappearing-ink fabric marker
(see Transferring Pattern
Markings in chapter 1 for
details).

2   If you're including pom-poms,
make them now (see Making
Pom-Poms following the Beach
Bag directions).

3   With right sides together, pin
the bag lining at the dots and
corners on one side seam. Pin
the other side seam. Sew the
side seams, leaving the area
between the dots unstitched,
and backstitch at both ends.
Press the seams flat, including
the area that is unstitched
(**Figure 1**).

4   With right sides together, match
the single notches on the lining
base with the side seams on
the lining bag. Then match the
double notches on the lining
base and lining bag. Pin around
the lining base, then sew with a
straight stitch. Clip the curve.
Press the seam allowance
toward the base (**Figure 2**).

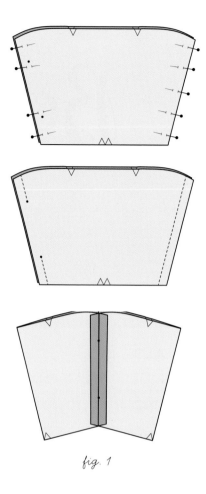

fig. 1

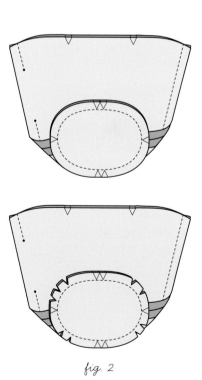

fig. 2

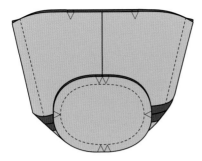

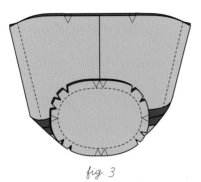

fig. 3

fig. 4

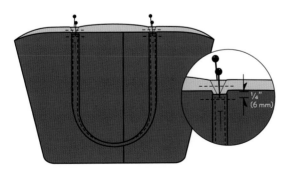

fig. 5

5 With right sides together on the main fabric, match and pin the side seams together. Sew the side seams with a straight stitch. With right sides together, match the single notches on the base with the side seams on the bag. Then match the double notches on the base and the bag. Pin around the base, then sew with a straight stitch. Clip the curve. Press the seam allowance toward the base (**Figure 3**).

6 Referring to **Figure 4**, fold the handles lengthwise with wrong sides together along the fold line and press. Fold the raw edges on the long sides toward the center fold to encase the raw edges, then press and pin along the folded edges. Topstitch through the layers on the outside edges.

7 Turn the main fabric right side out. With right sides together, pin each end of one handle on one side of the bag as shown, matching the notches on the handle and bag. Attach the handle ends with a scant ¼" (6 mm) seam (**Figure 5**). Repeat with the other handle on the other side of the bag.

8 Turn the main fabric wrong side out with the handles on the inside against the right side of the fabric. Place the lining inside the main fabric with right sides together matching the notches and side seams. Pin and sew the fabrics together along the upper edge (**Figure 6**).

9 Pull the lining up and turn the bag right side out through the opening (**Figure 7**).

10 Push the lining down into the bag and press. Pin and sew along the upper edge of the bag (**Figure 8**).

11 Through the layers, line up the base seams of the main fabric and lining (with the seam allowances folded toward the base) and pin the layers close to the base seams (**Figure 9**).

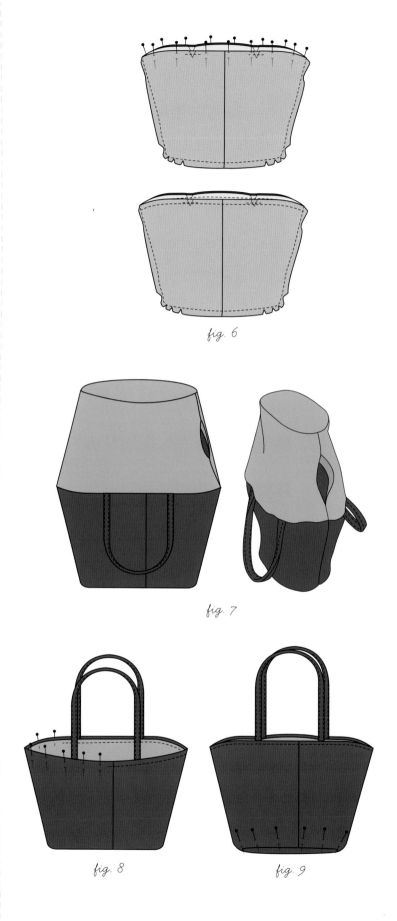

fig. 6

fig. 7

fig. 8

fig. 9

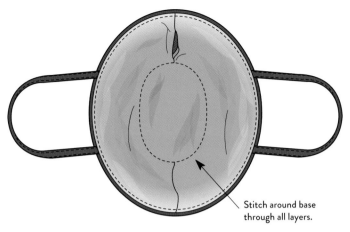

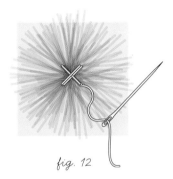

Stitch around base
through all layers.

fig. 10

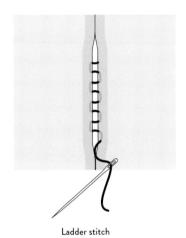

Ladder stitch

fig. 11

fig. 12

12 Push down the sides of the
bag flat to get the needle in
position, then sew the base
lining, stitching on the lining
through the layers around the
base (**Figure 10**).

13 Turn the bag inside out. Hand-
sew the opening in the lining
closed with a ladder stitch,
securing both ends (**Figure 11**).

14 Turn the bag right side out.
Youc an either hot glue or
handstitch each pom-pom on
the bag (**Figure 12**).

MAKING POM-POMS

MATERIALS

Yarn (see Pom-Pom Size tip to determine how much yarn is needed for your project)

2" (5 cm) elastic hair tie or elastic cording (optional)

Flat cardboard or plastic sheet, such as quilt template sheets or flat plastic packaging

Scissors (for cutting yarn as well as cardboard or plastic sheet)

Permanent marker

Sandpaper (sanding plastic sheets)

Pom-Pom pattern pieces: Small or Large (see downloadable template PDF)

Create fluffy pom-poms in a variety of yarn colors and textures to embellish your Beach Bag. You can also use them to decorate gifts, party hats, and more. Make a pom-pom template out of cardboard or a plastic sheet (for a more durable template to reuse over and over).

Tip: For a multi-color look, wrap different colors of yarn around the template in sections to create blocks of color.

1   Trace the pom-pom template onto the plastic sheet or cardboard twice. Cut out both templates. For plastic templates only, smooth the rough edges with sandpaper so the yarn doesn't snag.

2   Place the templates together. Referring to **Figure 1** and holding the end of one or more yarn colors, wrap the yarn around the joined templates in layers making passes from one end of the template to the other until the templates are full.

Note: The number of times it takes to wrap the yarn will depend on the thickness of the yarn. But in general, the more you wrap the yarn, the fuller the pom-pom.

3   Hold the layered yarn where the two ends of the template meet with your thumb and finger. Place the tip of the scissors between the two templates, then cut along the outside edge of the template (**Figure 2**). For more even strands, pull the scissors up toward the folded yarn edge while cutting.

Note: If you are using a cardboard template, it is easier to move your scissors along the side of the cardboard instead of between the layers.

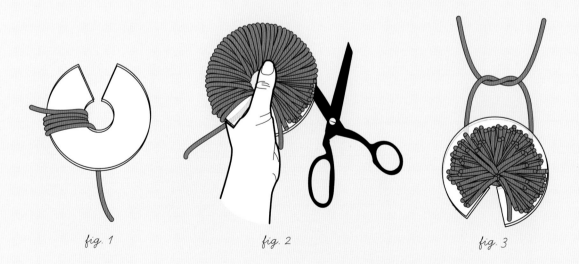

fig. 1   *fig. 2*   *fig. 3*

4   Wrap a single strand of yarn around the center of the pom-pom between the templates. Tie a double knot firmly at the center (**Figure 3**).

5   Remove the templates and fluff the pom-pom. Trim the ends to make the pom-pom round and even.

POM-POM SIZE

How thick you wrap the yarn around the templates will depend on how thick you want your pom-pom to be. The fullness also depends on how thick your yarn is. The process of making pom-poms is simple and forgiving, and they are cute in a variety of ways. So experiment to figure out the look you like. To make an extra small pom-pom, wrap the small template with yarn fifteen times and trim the pom-pom to size once it's made.

AT RIGHT: Turn your pom-pom into a hair accesosory or cheer pom-pom by stretching a 2" (5 cm) elastic hair tie around the center of the pom-pom between the two templates after completing step 4. Pinch the elastic in half, then wrap it around a finger to tie it into a knot close to the pom-pom center. Continue with step 5 to complete.

Athletic top

Contrasting shoulder panels give this top a sporty look. You can customize the front with a personalized design, such as the glittery star stencil shown here.

MATERIALS

Lightweight knit for main fabric, ¼ yard (0.2 m)

Contrasting lightweight knit for shoulder panels, ⅛ yard (11.5 cm)

Thread, coordinating with main fabric and the shoulder panel fabric

⅛" (3 mm) wide ribbon, 7–8" (18–20.5 cm)

Sew On Soft & Flexible Velcro, 4" (10 cm)

Wonder tape for ribbon (optional)

Stencil supplies (optional; see Making Stencils following the shirt directions)

Athletic Top pattern pieces: Front, Shoulder Panel 1, Shoulder Panel 2, Left Back, Right Back

All seam allowances are ¼" (6 mm) unless otherwise noted.

FABRIC NOTES

Main fabric: Use a knit with a stetch percentage that is anywhere from a low to a super-stretch. The fabric also needs a minimum of a 2-way stretch across the grain and good stretch recovery.

Contrasting fabric: Avoid fabric for the shoulder panels that has more stretch than the main fabric. For a different look, try sequin fabric with a knit backing or a fabric overlay such as lace or sequin fabric with a netting backing. (See the Lace Panel Shirt for directions on how to sew an overlay on a panel.)

UPCYCLE TIP

To get an athletic-wear look, use a repurposed T-shirt or a performance and swim knit.

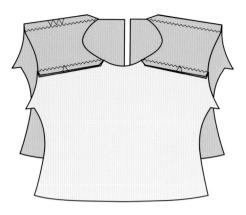

fig. 1

1   Using the pattern pieces,
    cut out the fabric.
    Transfer the notches on
    the pattern to the fabric
    with a disappearing-
    ink fabric marker (see
    Transferring Pattern
    Markings in chapter 1 for
    details).

    *Refer to **Figure 1** for steps 2
    and 3.*

2   With right sides together,
    match the single notch
    on each shoulder panel
    with the corresponding
    notch on the front piece
    and pin in place. Join the
    shoulder panels with a
    long, narrow zigzag stitch.

3   Place the left back and
    right back pieces right
    side up. Place the front
    piece on top, right side
    down. Match and pin the
    corresponding shoulder
    panels with the left and
    right back pieces and
    sew together with a long,
    narrow zigzag stitch.
    Press the shoulder seams
    toward the panel.

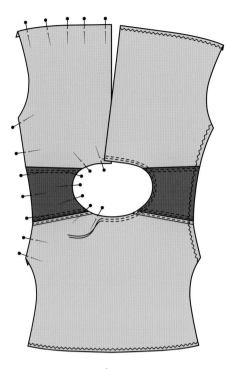

fig. 2

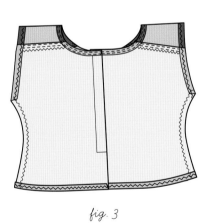

fig. 3

*Refer to **Figure 2** for steps 4–6.*

4 Cut a piece of ribbon to fit along the bottom edge of the front shoulder panel. Attach the ribbon with pins or strips of wonder tape, then straight stitch the ribbon in place. In the same manner, add ribbon to the other front shoulder seam.

5 With the fabric right side up, pin the seam allowance toward the shoulder panel along the seam lines. Sew with a long, narrow zigzag along the inside of the shoulder panel seam lines, catching the seam allowance on the back. Press flat.

6 Using a long, narrow zigzag stitch, finish the neckline, sleeve edges, and hemline with a single-fold hem. For tips, see Sewing Hems in chapter 1.

7 With right sides together, pin the front and back pieces together along the side seams. Sew with a long, narrow zigzag stitch (**Figure 3**).

8 Clip the curves, then turn the shirt right side out and press.

9 Add a Velcro closure on the back opening of the shirt (see Velcro Closures for Tops in chapter 1).

10 Decorate as desired.

MAKING STENCILS

MATERIALS

Fabric of your choice

Freezer paper

Clear tape

Masking tape

Scissors

Craft knife

Self-healing mat

Pencil

Iron and ironing board

Pressing cloth

Soft Fabric Paint (flexible fabric paint)

Dry sponge

Glitter

Glue for applying glitter to fabric (I like Tulip Fashion Glitter Bond because it's flexible)

Cardboard

Paper

Fabric markers

Stencils: Use the star, Cheer Squad, or numbers in the downloadable PDF or make your own

Freezer-Paper Stencils

Stencils are a fun way to personalize the fashions you sew. There are stencil templates in the downloadable PDF that comes with this book or you can create your own designs. You can also embellish stencils with fabric paint or markers and glitter. Test paint colors on the fabric you plan to use. Fabric paint is vibrant on white fabric, but some colors also cover well on colored fabric. Add glitter to get full coverage.

1   Tape a piece of freezer paper shiny-side down on a sheet of printer paper (this will keep it from getting jammed in the printer). Run the paper through your printer, copying the stencil template onto the freezer-paper side.

Note: Be sure to leave 1" (2.5 cm) margin around each shape.

2   Cut out the stencils, leaving a ½" (1.3 cm) border around each shape. Remove any tape and carefully cut out the center of the stencils with a craft knife, holding the paper down as you cut to keep it from tearing. Save all the tiny inside pieces.

3   Lay the fabric on an ironing board and press flat. Find the center of the project for a reference point, then arrange the freezer-paper stencils shiny-side down on the fabric. Be sure to place any small pieces.

4   With the iron on high and using a pressing cloth, if necessary, press the freezer-paper stencils on the fabric for 5 seconds per section. When it's cool, test the edges of the freezer paper to make sure it adhered. If not, press again.

TO GET THE LOOK OF THE ATHLETIC TOP WITH THE STAR STENCIL, USE BOTH THE OUTER AND INNER STAR TEMPLATES. PAINT THE PURPLE SECTION AND PINK SECTION, THEN ADD PURPLE AND PINK GLITTER. REMOVE THE TEMPLATE. LET THE STENCIL DRY COMPLETELY. THEN USE A BLACK FABRIC MARKER TO COLOR IN THE SPACE BETWEEN THE STARS.

Decorating stencils

1. Secure the fabric or garment to a piece of flat cardboard with masking tape along the edges to keep it from shifting while you paint.

2. Using a small, dry sponge, dab on thin layers of paint to cover the stencil but not leak under the edges.

3. Let the paint dry for about 10 minutes, or until it's dry to the touch. Add a second coat, if needed.

4. If you're adding glitter, place the fabric or garment on a piece of paper. Using a dry sponge, dab a layer of glue onto the fabric or garment. Sprinkle the glitter generously over the project. Gently lift the project to let the loose glitter fall off and pour the excess glitter back into the container. Repeat to add more colors. Let the glitter dry for about 10 minutes.

IF YOU ARE USING MULTIPLE COLORS OF GLITTER. POUR THE GLITTER INTO THE CREASE OF A FOLDED PIECE OF PAPER. THEN POUR THE GLITTER THROUGH THE FOLD TO DIRECT THE FLOW ONTO THE PROJECT.

5. Gently remove the freezer paper. If needed, use a pin to pick off the center of the freezer paper without disturbing the paint or glitter.

6. Lay the project flat and let the paint dry completely, preferably for about 24 hours.

7. When the project is dry to the touch, you can add details with a fabric marker.

Athletic shorts

Make these comfy athletic shorts out of a knit or woven fabric. The side panels are sporty and a fun way to add in details with a contrasting color or print. The shorts also features a soft knit waistband for easy on and off.

MATERIALS

Light- to medium-weight woven or knit for main fabric, ¼ yard (0.2 m)

Contrasting light- to medium-weight woven or knit for side panel, ⅛ yard (11.5 cm)

Light- to medium-weight knit for waistband, ⅛ yard (11.5 cm)

⅝" (1.5 cm) fold-over elastic, 10½" (26.5 cm) length

Thread: Coordinating with main fabric, contrasting fabric, and waistband (for less noticeable stitching, switch topstitching thread to match fabric)

Athletic Shorts pattern pieces: Front, Back, Side Panel; Waistband and Waistband Marking Guide

All seam allowances are ¼" (6 mm) unless otherwise noted.

FABRIC NOTES

Main fabric: Stretch is not necessary in the choice of fabric. If you choose a knit fabric, pick a substantial knit with good stretch recovery. For woven fabric, look for quilting cotton or a lightweight denim. My favorite fabric for the main body of the shorts is a T-shirt knit. Performance and swim knits are another option, since they are a great weight and usually easy to sew (use the matte side).

Side panel: Avoid fabrics with more stretch than the main fabric. For a different look, try sequins with a knit backing (see Sewing Sequin Fabric in chapter 1).

Waistband: The waistband is a casing for soft fold-over elastic, so the stretch amount is key to ensure the fabric and elastic stretch together. Stick to a moderate- to super-stretch lightweight knit with at least a 2-way stretch across the grain and great stretch recovery to reduce bulk. A T-shirt is a great option.

UPCYCLE TIP

Make these shorts from a repurposed T-shirt or leggings.

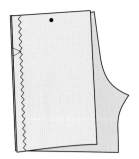

fig. 1

1   Using the pattern pieces, cut out the fabric. Transfer the notches and dots on the pattern to the fabric with a disappearing-ink fabric marker (see Transferring Marking Patterns in chapter 1).

2   With right sides together, match the notches on the front piece and the side panel. Pin the pieces together and zigzag stitch along the front side seam (**Figure 1**).

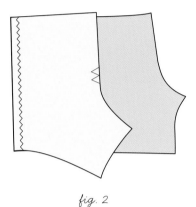

fig. 2

3   With right sides together, match and pin the back piece and side panel. Sew the pieces together with a regular zigzag stitch (**Figure 2**).

4   Trim the seam allowances and press toward the center panel (**Figure 3**). To flatten the seams, turn the fabric right side up and pin the seam allowance through the layers. Topstitch with a long, narrow zigzag stitch next to the seam on the center panel.

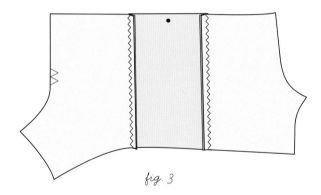

fig. 3

5   Repeat steps 2–4 with the other front, back, and side panel pieces.

6   Hem each leg of the shorts, using a single fold hem for knits or a double-fold hem for wovens (see Sewing Hems in chapter 1 for directions).

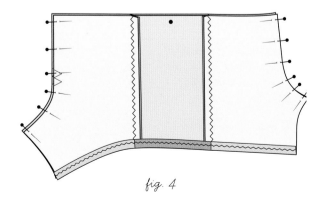

fig. 4

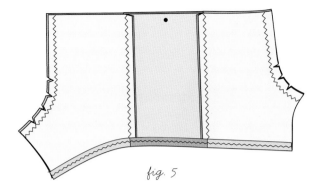

fig. 5

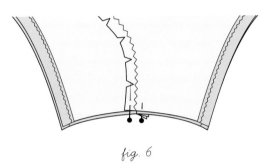

fig. 6

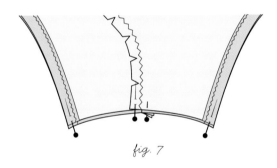

fig. 7

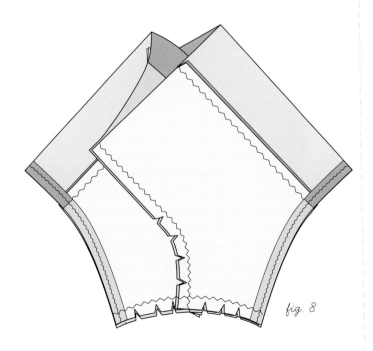

fig. 8

7 With right sides together, match and pin the center front to the center back (**Figure 4**). Sew the center front and center back with a zigzag stitch. Clip the seam allowance at the curve (**Figure 5**).

8 With right sides together, refold the shorts, matching the front to the back. Match and pin the front and back inseam at the center seam. Pin the front center seam allowance and back center seam allowance in opposite directions (**Figure 6**).

9 Match and pin the front and back inseam hems. Pin along the inseam (**Figure 7**). Stitch along the inseam, then clip the curve (**Figure 8**).

10 Turn the shorts right side out and press the inseam, center front, and center back.

11 Add the waistband to complete the shorts (see Adding a Knit Waistband in chapter 1 for details).

TO MAKE THE SHORTS WITHOUT THE SIDE PANEL, TAPE THE FRONT, SIDE, AND BACK PATTERN PIECES TOGETHER WITH THE PIECES OVERLAPPING AND THE SEAM LINES MATCHING UP. CUT OUT THE PATTERN PIECE AS ONE UNIT. CUT TWO PANELS FROM THE FABRIC WITH THE NEW PATTERN PIECE. THEN FOLLOW STEPS 6–11 TO MAKE THE SHORTS.

Heart top

This shirt features a hi-low hemline and a connected sleeve. It is an over-the-head style with no Velcro closures, making it a quick sew. Also included is a heart appliqué for a fun and easy-to-add embellishment.

MATERIALS

Light- to medium-weight super-stretch knit, ¼ yard (0.2 m)

Light- to medium-weight heat-tolerant knit for the heart appliqué, ⅛ yard (11.5 cm)

Double needle for hems (optional)

Thread: 2 spools coordinating with fabric, 1 spool coordinating with heart (if you're using a double needle for the single-fold hem)

Iron-on adhesive, such as HeatnBond Lite (recommended but optional)

Heart Top pattern pieces: Front, Back, Appliqué template (heart template included)

All seam allowances are ¼" (6 mm) unless otherwise noted.

FABRIC NOTES

Main fabric: This pattern requires fabric with a lot of stretch! Use a 4-way super-stretch fabric with good stretch recovery. (See Fabric Notes in chapter 1 for tips.)

Appliqué fabric: Use a knit fabric for no-fray edges. Any stretch percentage from low to super stretch will work. Add a little pizzazz with a shiny performance-knit fabric. Once you've ironed on the appliqué you can stitch an overlay fabric onto the appliqué that is not heat-tolerant, such as sequin fabric, and special occasion fabric with a no-fray netting or knit backing. Cut the overlay fabric using your appliqué template, pin, and straight stitch in place.

1   Using the pattern pieces, cut out the fabric. Transfer the notches on the pattern to the fabric with a disappearing-ink fabric marker (see Transferring Pattern Markings in chapter 1 for details).

2   With right sides together, match the notches on the front and back shoulder. Pin the front and back fabric pieces together along the shoulder seams. Sew with a regular zigzag stitch (**Figure 1**). Trim the seam allowance and the press seams flat.

3   Switch to a double needle. Use the directions for Single-Fold Hem with a Double Needle in chapter 1 to finish the edges of the sleeves, hemline, and neckline (**Figure 2**).

    Note: You can also finish the edges with a single-fold hem with a regular zigzag stitch using a single needle (see Sewing Hems in chapter 1).

4   Switch back to a single needle. With right sides together, pin front and back side seams. Using a regular zigzag stitch, sew the side seams (**Figure 3**). Trim the seam allowance and clip the curve. Turn the shirt right side out and press.

5   If desired, add the appliqué heart (see Creating Iron-on Designs for directions).

fig. 1

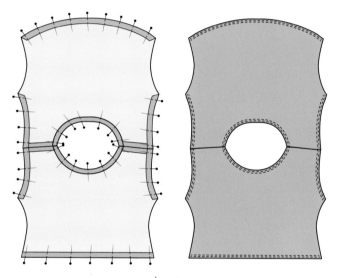

fig. 2

fig. 3

CREATING IRON-ON DESIGNS

MATERIALS

Heat-tolerant fabric

Coordinating thread

Iron-on adhesive

Pins

Scissors

Pencil

Iron

Pressing sheets to protect fabric from heat and iron from adhesive (optional)

Heart appliqué template (create your own or download our version at www.quiltingcompany.com/MyDollMyStyleTemplates)

This method uses an iron-on adhesive to hold the appliqué shape to the fabric while you sew around it. I like HeatnBond Lite because it uses low heat and short pressing times, so it can be used on a variety of fabrics. When choosing a design to appliqué, pick a fairly simple shape, so it's easy to stitch around on your sewing machine. You can also cut out simple designs from printed fabric to appliqué.

1 Trace the appliqué template on the paper side of the iron-on adhesive.

   Note: If the direction of your shape is important, take care to trace the mirror image of your shape.

2 Cut out a square shape around the design. Place the paper square adhesive-side down on the wrong side of the fabric, making sure it doesn't overhang the fabric. Adhere the iron-on adhesive to the fabric following the manufacturer's directions (**Figure 1**).

3 Using pins, mark the placement of the shape on the garment you want to adhere it to.

4 Cut out the shape through the fabric and paper. Peel off the paper backing (the adhesive will be on the wrong side of the fabric shape) and place the shape adhesive-side down on the garment. Follow the manufacturer's directions for attaching the shape (**Figure 2**).

   Note: To center the heart, fold the shirt in half to find the center and place a pin. Then measure 1" (2.5 cm) down from the center of the neckline to place the heart.

5 Straight stitch around the shape with a matching thread (**Figure 3**).

fig. 1

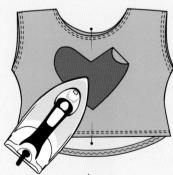

fig. 2

fig. 3

Textured skirt

This A-line skirt is designed with a simple shape so you can add a lovely textured special-occasion fabric. These fancy fabrics are fun to sew and make sweet, fashionable skirts. You can sew up a variety of looks depending on the fabric you choose. Transparent fabrics such as mesh, lace, or sequin fabric with a netting backing will need a skirt lining. There are also three ways to finish the hem on the skirt. Use an unfinished hem for no-fray fabrics. A lace or trim-edged hem will add a nice design detail. A single-fold hem offers a sweet, simple finish for fabrics with a little fray.

MATERIALS

Light- or medium-weight knit, open-weave knit, mesh, tulle, lace, sequin fabric, and special-occasion fabrics with no-fray backing, ¼ yard (0.2 m)

Lightweight knit for lining (optional), ⅛ yard (11.5 cm)

Coordinating thread (with main fabric)

¼" (6 mm) pom-pom or lace trim (optional), 16½" (42 cm)

⅝" (1.5 cm) fold-over elastic, 10½" (26.5 cm) length

Textured Skirt pattern pieces: Front and Back

All seam allowances are ¼" (6 mm) unless otherwise noted.

FABRIC NOTES

Main fabric: Textured special-occasion fabric often has a top layer such as sequins, embroidery, or 3-D flowers on backing material. Both layers should be no-fray. Good backing options include knits and netting fabrics with a little stretch. For an all-lace skirt, use a soft lace that has at least some stretch.

Lining fabric: Use fabric with a stretch percentage that is anywhere from low to super stretch with at least a 2-way stretch across the grain in a coordinating or contrasting color to the outer skirt.

UPCYCLE TIP

Use a T-shirt for the skirt lining. You can find great colors to match with your fun textured special-occasion fabric.

1   Using the pattern pieces, cut out the fabric. Cut out the front and back pieces from the lining material, if including. Transfer the dots on the pattern to the fabric with a disappearing-ink fabric marker (see Transferring Pattern Markings in chapter 1 for details).

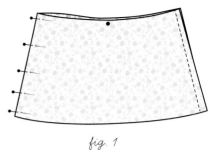

fig. 1

2   With right sides together, pin the front and back main pieces together along the side seams. Sew with a straight stitch or long, narrow zigzag stitch. Trim the seam allowance (**Figure 1**). In the same way, sew the lining pieces together (**Figure 2**).

3   Turn the skirt and lining right side out. Place the lining inside the skirt with the side seams pressed toward the back. Pin the fabric together at the dots and side seams (**Figure 3**).

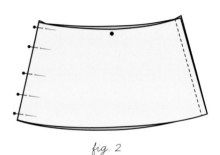

fig. 2

4   Fold the elastic in half lengthwise with right sides together, lining up the short ends. Pin and sew the ends together with a straight stitch. Press the seam open. Fold the elastic into quarters and mark (with dots) with the seam at one mark.

fig. 3

5   With right sides together, match the seam in the elastic with the dot on the skirt back and pin. Match and pin the three remaining dots on the elastic with the skirt side seams and the front dot. Pin the elastic to the skirt between the markings. Sew with a regular zigzag stitch on the edge of the elastic with no seam allowance (**Figure 4**).

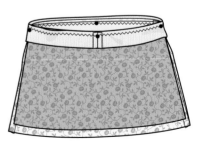

fig. 4

6 Turn the elastic to the right side. Fold the seam allowance toward the skirt and pin the seam allowance through the layers on the right side of the fabric. Topstitch on the skirt using a long, narrow zigzag stitch for fabrics with little to no stretch and a regular zigzag stitch on fabrics with medium to high stretch.

7 Finish the hem using one of the following options:

Unfinished hemline: If you used no-fray fabrics, the skirt is done!

Lace or trim hemline: With right sides together, fold the lace or trim in half. Match up the ends, then pin and stitch them together. Fold the lace into quarters and mark (with dots) with the seam at one mark. Fold the skirt edge into quarters and mark (with dots) the center front, center back, and side seams. With the right sides out, match the dots on the lace with the dots on the skirt edge, then overlap the lace on the skirt edge and pin it to the skirt at the side seams, front, and back with the lace seam at the center back. Place more pins around the skirt edge to secure the lace, then sew the lace to the edge with a regular zigzag stitch. Trim the skirt in the seam allowance and press.

Single-fold hemline: See Sewing Hems in chapter 1.

Flutter sleeve dress

This summery frock features many fun details, including gathered flutter sleeves and a gathered dress ruffle. There is also an optional lace overlay on the bodice. This project is slightly more advanced than others in the book and may be challenging for a beginner, but this gorgeous dress is worth the effort.

MATERIALS

Lightweight knit for the main fabric, ¼ yard (0.2 m)

Lightweight lace for the overlay, ⅛ yard (11.5 cm)

Thread: Coordinating with main fabric and lace

Sew On Soft & Flexible Velcro, 5" (12.5 cm) length

Wonder tape (optional)

Flutter Sleeve Dress pattern pieces: Upper Bodice Front, Upper Bodice Back, Lower Bodice Front, Lower Bodice Back, Side Front, Side Back, Flutter Sleeve Ruffle, Dress Ruffle

Note: This pattern shares pattern pieces with the Flutter Sleeve Tunic.

All seam allowances are ¼" (6 mm) unless otherwise noted.

FABRIC NOTES

Main fabric: Use a knit fabric with a stretch percentage anywhere from a low to super stretch with at least a 2-way stretch across the grain and good stretch recovery.

Fabric overlay: Use a lightweight or stretch lace with anywhere from a low stretch to super stretch and at least a 2-way stretch across the grain. You can use a matching lace from a repurposed shirt or, for a different look, use a contrasting fabric for the overlay.

UPCYCLE TIP

This is a great pattern to make from a repurposed T-shirt.

1   Using the pattern pieces, cut out the fabric. Transfer the notches and dots on the pattern to the fabric with a disappearing-ink fabric marker (see Transferring Pattern Markings in chapter 1).

2   Pin a Side Front and a Side Back together at the shoulders with right sides together. Sew a regular zigzag stitch along the shoulder, then trim the seam allowance. Sew a single-fold hem with a zigzag stitch along the armhole opening to finish the edge (**Figure 1**). Repeat for the other Side Front and Side Back pieces.

3   Referring to the Ruffle Pattern in the Templates section, pin and sew a single-fold hem with a narrow, long zigzag stitch on the long edge of a Sleeve Ruffle opposite the gather lines. Stitch the gather lines on the Sleeve Ruffle ¼" (6 mm) and ⅛" (3 mm) from the edge with a long straight stitch and no backstitches, leaving about a 4" (10 cm) long tail on each end.

4   With right sides up, match the Sleeve Ruffle notch and the Side Front notch. Gather the ruffle by pulling the bobbin threads until the ruffle is equal to the distance between the squares on the Side Front and Back unit.

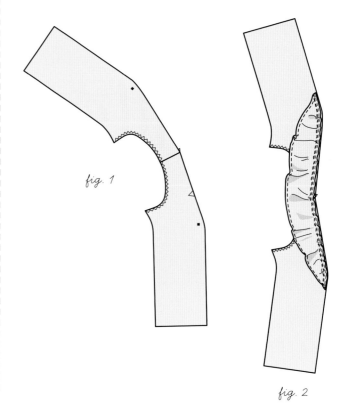

fig. 1

fig. 2

fig. 3

5 Referring to **Figure 2** and with right sides up, match the center dot on the Sleeve Ruffle with the side shoulder seam and pin. Match and pin the ruffle point on each end of the ruffle with the dot on the Side Front and Side Back units as shown on the pattern. Adjust the ruffle gathers by pulling the bobbin threads between the two points, then pin in place. Straight stitch the ruffle from point to point.

6 Follow steps 3–5 to hem, gather, and sew the Sleeve Ruffle on the other Side Front and Back unit.

Refer to **Figure 3** *for steps 7–9*

7 With right sides up, pin the lace overlay on the Upper Bodice Front main fabric. Baste around the sides and bottom, then use a regular zigzag stitch along the edge of the neckline (with no seam allowance).

8 Stitch the gather lines on the Lower Bodice Front ¼" (6 mm) and ⅛" (3 mm) from the edge with a long straight stitch and no backstitches, leaving about a 4" (10 cm) long tail on each end.

9 Arrange the Lower Bodice Front and Upper Bodice Front with right sides up, then gather the Lower Bodice Front by pulling the bobbin thread until it's roughly the width of the Upper Bodice Front.

10 Match and pin the edge of the Upper Bodice Front to the top edge of the gathered Lower Bodice Front with right sides together. Sew with a straight stitch. Press the seam allowance toward the upper bodice. Pin along the seam line on the right side of the Upper Bodice Front, then topstitch through the seam allowance with a straight stitch.

11 Line up and pin the Upper Bodice Back and the Lower Bodice Back with right sides together, then sew with a regular zigzag stitch. Trim the seam allowance. Place the unit flat with the seam allowance toward the upper bodice, then pin along the seam line on the right side of the fabric. Sew a long, narrow zigzag stitch on the upper bodice next to the seam.

12 Repeat steps 10 and 11 with the other Upper Bodice Back and Lower Bodice Back pieces (**Figure 4**).

13 Line up and pin the Front and Back Bodice units together at the shoulders with right sides together. Pin the shoulders together, then sew with a regular zigzag stitch. Trim the seam allowance (**Figure 5**).

14 Following the directions in Sewing Hems in chapter 1, sew a single-fold hem around the neckline using a long, narrow zigzag stitch or a double needle.

15 With right sides together, match the notches on the Side unit with the notches on the Upper Bodice Front. Pin at the ends and the shoulder seam. Then match and pin the square marking guides on the side piece with the seam on the Upper/Lower Bodice Front and Upper/Lower Bodice Back units.

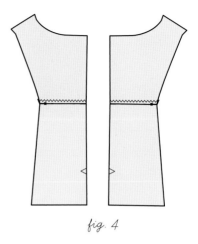

fig. 4

fig. 5

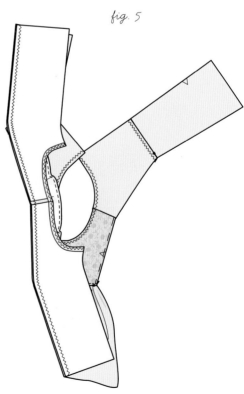

fig. 6

Pin along the side and sew together with a regular zigzag stitch (**Figure 6**). Open flat and press the seams.

16 Pin the seam along the length of the sleeve ruffle with the seam allowance toward the Bodice Front and Back. Topstitch through the layers, including the seam allowance, the length of the ruffle on the bodice front and back.

17 Repeat steps 15 and 16 for the second Side unit (**Figure 7**).

18 Add the Velcro closure and stitch the center back (see Velcro Closures for Tunics and Dresses in chapter 1).

19 Stitch the gather lines on the Dress Ruffle at ¼" (6 mm) and ⅛" (3 mm) from the edge with a long straight stitch and no backstitches, leaving about a 4" (10 cm) tail on either end. Pull the two bobbin threads to gather the ruffle to the width of the dress front (refer to **Figure 3** when gathering the Dress Ruffle and matching the edges to the front unit). With right sides together, pin the gathered edge of the ruffle to the bottom edge of the front. Sew the pieces together with a straight stitch. Turn the dress right-side out with the seam allowance on the wrong side folded up, away from the dress ruffle. Pin along the upper edge of the seam from the right side catching the seam allowance on the wrong side. Topstitch with a straight stitch catching the seam allowance.

20 Repeat step 19 to create a second dress ruffle and sew it on the back unit.

21 Match the front and back with right sides together. Pin along the side seams, then sew with a regular zigzag stitch. Trim the seam allowance.

22 Turn the dress right side out. Sew a single-fold hem with a long, narrow zigzag stitch on the dress ruffle (see Single-Fold Hem with a Zigzag Stitch in chapter 1 for more details).

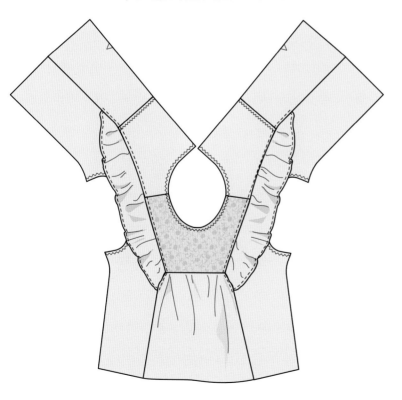

fig. 7

Flutter sleeve tunic

With these directions, you can turn the Flutter Sleeve Dress into a cute top. It looks great with the Athletic Shorts or a pair of Leggings (see Leggings and Jeggings). The optional trim is a fun detail that gives the tunic extra style.

MATERIALS

Lightweight knit, ¼ yard (0.2 m)

Lightweight lace for the overlay, ¼ yard (0.2 m)

Thread: Coordinating with main fabric and the lace overlay fabric.

Sew On Soft & Flexible Velcro, 4" (10 cm)

Wonder tape

Flutter Sleeve Tunic pattern pieces: Upper Bodice Front, Upper Bodice Back, Lower Bodice Front, Lower Bodice Back, Side Front, Side Back, Flutter Sleeve Ruffle

Note: This pattern shares pattern pieces with the Flutter Sleeve Dress.

All seam allowances are ¼" (6 mm) unless otherwise noted.

FABRIC NOTES

Main fabric: Use a knit fabric with a stretch percentage that is at least low stretch with 2-way stretch across the grain with great stretch recovery. A good place to find knits with matching lace and trim is in repurposed shirts.

Overlay fabric: Use a lace fabric that has at least a low stretch percentage and 2-way stretch across the grain.

UPCYCLE TIP

This is a great pattern to make from a repurposed T-shirt.

1   Follow steps 1–17 of the Flutter Sleeve dress (**Figure 1**).

2   Add the 4" (10 cm) Velcro closure to the back of the shirt: Refer to Velcro Closures for Tops in chapter 1 for directions, following step 1 to sew on the Velcro. Next, match, pin, and stitch the fabric ⅜" (1 cm) below the Velcro (parallel to the bottom edge of the Velcro). From that seam line, stitch along the center back to the bottom edge of the tunic with a ⅜" (1 cm) seam allowance. Follow step 5–6 to complete the closure.

3   Lay the front and back pieces with right sides together. Pin the side seams and sew with a regular zigzag stitch.

4   Finish the hem using one of the following options:

   Single-Fold Hemline: See Sewing Hems in chapter 1.

   Trim hemline: Lay the shirt right side up. With right sides together, match and pin the trim edge with the cut edge of the tunic hemline with the pom-poms facing up. Use a regular zigzag stitch on the trim along the edge (with no seam allowance). Fold down the trim to the right side (**Figure 2**). Pin the seam with the seam allowance toward the fabric and topstitch with a straight stitch on the fabric catching the seam allowance in the stitches.

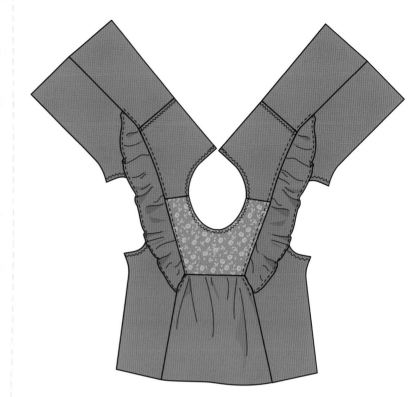

fig. 1

fig. 2

OPPOSITE: The Flutter Sleeve Tunic (left) and Flutter Sleeve Dress (right) share pattern pieces, but the finished looks can be customized for your doll.

Fringe purse

This purse features three rows of fringe on the front with a band of ribbon or trim across the front and back. Be sure to cut the three layers of fringe all at once (see the project directions for tips). For a variation, leave the purse front plain or cover it in strips of ribbon and trim.

MATERIALS

Faux leather for main fabric, ¼ yard (0.2 m)

Woven fabric for lining, ¼ yard (0.2 m)

Microtex (Sharp) needle for faux leather

Thread: Coordinating with main fabric, lining, and ribbon

½" (1.3 cm) wide ribbon or trim, 8" (20.5 cm) length cut into (2) 4" (10 cm) segments

Wonder tape

Clear ruler

Fringe Purse pattern pieces: Front/Back (1 piece), Lining, Handle 1, Handle 2, Fringe 1, Fringe 2, Fringe 3, Fringe Cutting Guide

All seam allowances are ¼" (6 mm) unless otherwise noted.

FABRIC NOTES

Main fabric: Light- to medium-weight faux leather, pleather, or vinyl is perfect for making fringe and doll purses, and it doesn't fray.

Lining fabric: Choose a lightweight woven, such as quilting cotton, with a fun print.

1   Using the pattern pieces, cut out the fabric. Transfer the dots on the pattern to the fabric with a disappearing-ink fabric marker. Then mark the ribbon and fringe placement lines on the purse Front and Back using the pattern as a guide.

2   Make the fringe using the Purse Fringe Cutting Guide in the templates PDF and referring to the Fool-Proof Fringe directions (see the Fringe Swimsuit). The purse has three lengths of fringe, so be sure to cut all three layers at the same time with the longest layer on top (**Figure 1**).

3   Layer the three fringe pieces on the front of the purse with the longest on the bottom and the shortest on the top, lining up the top edges and holding them together with wonder tape or pins. Place the fringe as shown on the pattern, lining it up with the placement lines.

4   Sew across the top of all three layers of fringe with ¼" (6 mm) seam allowance. Trim the seam allowance at different levels as shown to reduce bulk (**Figure 2**).

5   Arrange ribbon along both placement lines on the short sides of the purse (one is also lined up with the top edge of the fringe), then edgestitch around the ribbon (**Figure 3**).

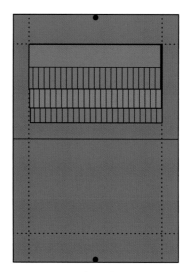

fig. 1

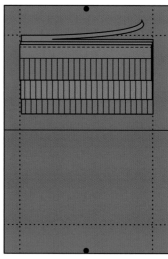

fig. 2

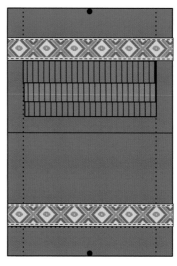

fig. 3

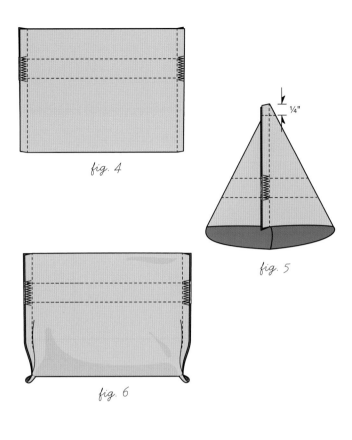

fig. 4

fig. 5

fig. 6

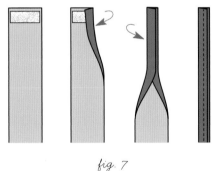

fig. 7

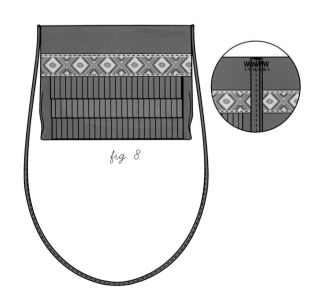

fig. 8

5   Fold the purse along the fold line (see the pattern) with right sides together, matching the ribbon on the edges, and pin in place. Using a straight stitch, sew the sides. Then zigzag stitch over the ribbon ends next to the seam (**Figure 4**). Trim the seam allowance.

6   Referring to **Figure 5**, hold the purse with the side seam facing you and the bottom corner up. Pinch the bottom corner forming a triangle with the seam in the center, then lay the corner flat. Measure ¼" (6 mm) from the tip of the corner and mark a line perpendicular to the side seam line. Stitch along the line. Repeat with the other bottom corner (**Figure 6**). Turn purse right side out.

7   Fold the handle piece lengthwise into thirds. For an alternative to pins, use a strip of wonder tape on the end to get started. Stitch the handle lengthwise, folding and stitching as you go (**Figure 7**).

8   With right sides together, place one end of the handle centered on one side seam and attach with pins or wonder tape. With the purse right side out, straight stitch the handle to the purse and zigzag stitch in the seam allowance to reinforce the seam. Repeat to attach the other end of the handle to the side seam (**Figure 8**).

9 With right sides together, pin the lining pieces together at the dots and along the side seams. Stitch from each bottom dot toward the corner and up the side seam, then carefully trim the seam allowance on the side seams slightly (**Figure 9**).

10 Following the directions in step 6 for the main fabric, stitch the corners of the lining (**Figure 10**).

11 Lay the lining down with the wrong side out. Lay the purse right side out, then push the handle inside the lining, followed by the purse. With the purse and lining now right sides together, match the center squares and side seams of the lining and purse. Pin the pieces together on either side of the handles and at the center squares, then pin around the opening to secure. Place the sewing machine needle inside the opening edge and stitch ¼" (6 mm) on the wrong side of the purse (**Figure 11**).

12 Turn the purse right side out by pulling the purse through the space between the dots on the lining.

13 With the lining turned right side out, fold the fabric under ¼" (6 mm) between the dots and press. Pin the fabric, then finish with an edgestitch.

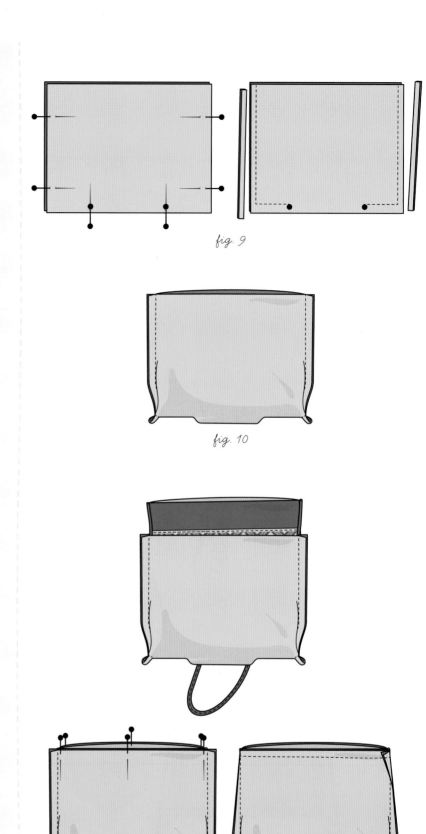

fig. 9

fig. 10

fig. 11

fig. 12

14 Push the lining into the purse and pin along the purse opening, pulling the lining down into the purse ⅛" (3 mm). Switch the thread so the main thread matches the lining and the bobbin matches the purse. Place the purse opening edge under the sewing machine needle and edge stitch the lining around the purse opening (**Figure 12**).

Lace panel top

This top features a dolman-style sleeve with a panel for a lace overlay or contrasting fabric. Style this top for everyday wear with a variety of looks using different fabric combinations or pair it with cozy Pajama Pants for a stylish sleepover set. For a fun touch, paint polka dots on the lace overlay before you start sewing as shown here (see the included Printing Polka Dots directions).

MATERIALS

Lightweight knit for main fabric, ¼ yard (0.2 m)

Overlay fabric (lace shown here), ⅛ yard (11.5 cm)

Double needle (optional)

Thread: 2 spools for the double needle coordinating with main fabric and the front panel fabric (optional)

Sew On Soft & Flexible Velcro, 4" (10.5 cm) length

Soft fabric paint, cardboard, and pencil for polka dots (optional)

Lace Panel Top pattern pieces: Front, Front Panel, Back Right, Back Left

All seam allowances are ¼" (6 mm) unless otherwise noted.

FABRIC NOTES

Main fabric: This style calls for a minimum of both a low stretch percentage and a 2-way stretch across the grain plus great stretch recovery. You can use a repurposed T-shirt for a sleep shirt or use a performance knit or swim knit for a more athletic style. Instead of a lace overlay in the front panel, you can choose a solid or patterned knit for a color-block look or dress it up with sequin fabric with a knit backing.

Overlay fabric: Use a lightweight lace with at least a 2-way stretch across the grain. You can also use a sequin overlay with netting backing.

UPCYCLE TIP

This is a great pattern to make from a repurposed T-shirt.

1   Using the pattern pieces, cut out the fabric. Transfer the notches on the pattern to the fabric with a disappearing-ink fabric marker (see Transferring Pattern Markings in chapter 1).

2   Place the overlay fabric on the main fabric Front Panel with right sides up. Pin together along the edge and baste around the edges with a scant ¼" (6 mm) seam allowance (**Figure 1**).

3   With right sides together, pin the bottom of the Front Panel to the top of the Front piece. Sew along the edge with a long, narrow zigzag stitch and trim the seam allowance (**Figure 2**).

fig. 1

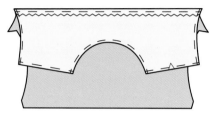

fig. 2

PRINTING POLKA DOTS

Polka dots are a fun addition to any project made with lace. The lace hides any stamping imperfections, and the stamp gives the lace a playful look.

Place the lace fabric on a flat cardboard surface. Lightly dip the top of a pencil eraser in a shallow puddle of soft fabric paint, then carefully stamp it on the fabric. Repeat to create the desired polka dot pattern. For semitransparent fabrics such as lace, blot the paint with a piece of paper on the fabric to pick up any extra paint. If you want a more vibrant color, restamp the polka dots with a second coat of paint. Allow the paint to dry flat for 4 hours.

PRACTICE STAMPING DOTS ON THE CARDBOARD TO FIGURE OUT HOW MUCH PAINT TO USE. THEN TEST ON A PIECE OF SCRAP FABRIC BEFORE YOU BEGIN.

4 Lay the Front unit flat with the right side up and the seam allowance folded away from the front panel. Press the front seam line and pin. (Finger-press if the fabric is not heat tolerant.) Switch to a double needle and stitch across the Front either below or straddling the seam line (match one thread to the main fabric and one to the lace if you straddle the seam line). Press the seam.

Note: You can also use a long, narrow zigzag stitch with a single needle above the seam line to hide the stitches in the lace.

5 Switch back to a single needle. With right sides together and matching notches, pin the front and back pieces together along the shoulder seams. Sew the pieces together with a regular zigzag stitch, then press the shoulder seams toward the back (**Figure 3**).

6 Switch to a double needle. Following the directions for sewing a Single-Fold Hem with a Double Needle in chapter 1, finish the sleeve edges, hemline, and neckline. Press the seams.

Note: You can also finish the edges with a Single-Fold Hem with a Zigzag Stitch (using a single needle).

7 Switch to a single needle. With right sides together, pin the front and back side seams together and sew with a regular zigzag stitch. Trim the seam allowance (**Figure 4**).

8 Turn the shirt right side out and press.

9 Add the Velcro closure to the back opening (see Velcro Closures for Tops in chapter 1 for details).

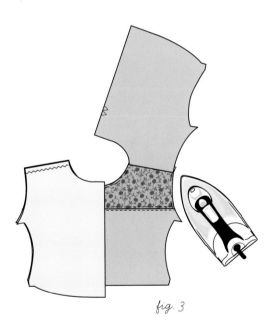

fig. 3

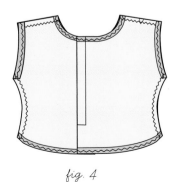

fig. 4

Pajama pants

This is a two-in-one pattern. With a slight adjustment to the cuff, you can sew either straight-leg pajama pants or modern jogger-style bottoms (instructions for both are included). Both styles feature a soft knit waistband for easy on and off and functional slant pockets. You can outline the pockets with decorative topstitching or, for the straight-leg pants, add pom-pom trim on the pocket opening or along the hem.

MATERIALS

Light- to medium-weight woven, ¼ yard (0.2 m)

Lightweight knit for the waistband, ⅛ yard (11.5 cm)

Thread: Coordinating with main fabric and waistband, and contrasting thread for topstitching (optional)

¼" (6 mm) trim, 20" (51 cm) length

⅝" (1.5 cm) fold-over elastic, 10½" (26.5 cm) length

Pajama Pants pattern pieces: Front, Back, Pocket Lining, Pocket, Leg Cuff (optional for jogger style); Waistband and Waistband Marking Guide

All seam allowances are ¼" (6 mm) unless otherwise noted.

FABRIC NOTES

Main fabric: For traditional PJ pants, use cozy flannel or lightweight quilting cotton. The jogger-style pants work better in a quilting cotton or a cotton shirting. For a quick, easy finish that minimizes fray, trim seam allowances and curves with pinking shears.

Waistband & cuff: The waistband is a casing for the soft fold-over elastic. The stretch amount is key so the fabric and elastic stretch together. Stick to a lightweight knit with moderate to super stretch and great stretch recovery to reduce bulk at the waistband. A repurposed T-shirt is a great option.

1   Using the pattern pieces, cut out the fabric. Transfer the notches on the pattern to the fabric with a disappearing-ink fabric marker (see Transferring Pattern Markings in chapter 1 for tips).

2   With right sides together, pin one Pocket Lining to the corresponding front leg along the pocket opening and sew with a straight stitch along the pocket opening (**Figure 1**).

3   Fold the Pocket Lining to the wrong side of the Front, matching the notches. Press the seam. Pin the layers together along the seam, then topstitch along the pocket opening with matching thread or contrasting thread depending on the look you want (**Figure 2**).

4   Repeat steps 1–3 with the other Pocket, Pocket Lining, and Front pieces.

5   If you want to add trim to the pocket (optional), cut a 3" (7.5 cm) segment of trim. Pin and sew it along the inside of the finished edge (**Figure 3**). Repeat for the other pocket.

6   With right sides together, match the notches on the Pocket with

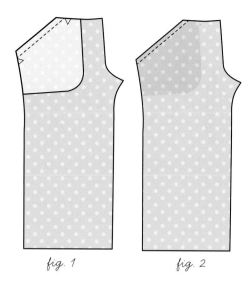

fig. 1   *fig. 2*

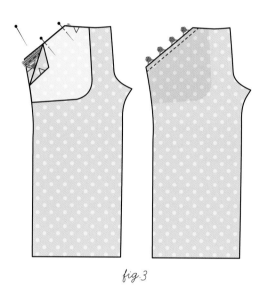

fig. 3

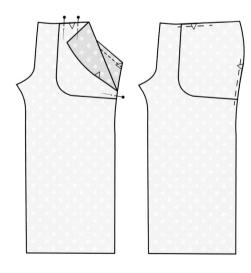

fig. 4

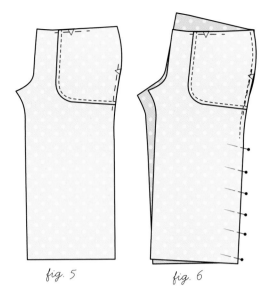

fig. 5   fig. 6

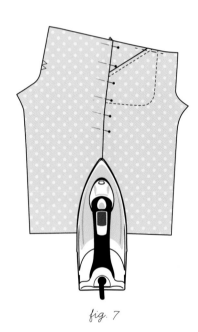

fig. 7

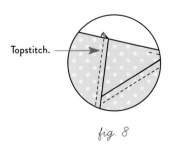

Topstitch. ——→

fig. 8

the notches on the Pocket Lining and pants front. Pin and baste the pieces together along the side seam and waist (**Figure 4**).

7   On the wrong side of the pants front, pin around the pocket bag to attach the pocket to the pants front. Sew around the pocket from the side seam to the waist with a regular straight stitch (**Figure 5**), using a matching thread for a subtle look or a contrasting thread to emphasize the pocket details.

8   Repeat steps 6 and 7 with the other Pocket, Pocket Lining, and Front pieces.

9   With right sides together, pin and sew a Front and Back piece together along the side seams, using a straight stitch (**Figure 6**).

10 Clip the curve in the seam allowance. With the fabric right side up, press the seam flat with the seam allowance folded toward the back. Pin the seam allowance through the layers on the right side of the fabric. (**Figure 7**).

11 Topstitch along the inside of the back side seam anchoring the seam allowance (**Figure 8**).

12 Repeat steps 9–11 with the other Front and Back piece.

13 Hem the pants using one of the following options:

Double-fold hem for straight-leg pants: Finish each pant leg with a double-fold hem (see Double-Fold Hem in chapter 1).

Add trim to straight-leg pants: Cut a 7" (18 cm) segment of trim for each pant leg, then sew the trim to the inside edge of each finished hem (**Figure 9**).

Jogger style cuff: See Sewing a Jogger Cuff for directions.

fig. 9

14 Place the front and back pieces with right sides together. Match the double notches on the center back together and pin. Line up and pin the center front together. Sew the center front and back seams, then clip the curves (**Figure 10**).

fig. 10

15 With right sides together and referring to **Figure 11**, pin the front and back center seam allowances together (pin in opposite directions to reduce bulk). Pin the front and back inseam hems and along the inseam. (For the jogger-style pants, pin the leg cuffs and then along the inseam.) Sew along the inseam and clip the curve.

16 Turn the pants right side out and press the inseam and the center front and back.

17 Add the waistband (see Adding a Knit Waistband in chapter 1 for directions).

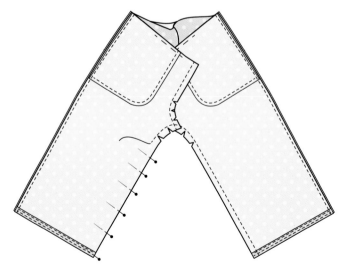

fig. 11

SEWING A JOGGER CUFF

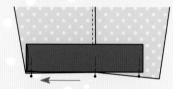

fig. a

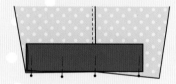

fig. b

fig. c

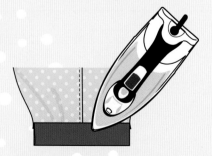

fig. d

1   Fold the pant cuff piece in half lengthwise and pin each end. Find the center by folding the cuff in half matching the ends and mark the center with a pin.

2   With right sides together, line up the open edge of the cuff with the bottom of a pant leg. Pin the center of the cuff to the side seam, then pin each side of the cuff to the edge of the pant leg as shown **(Figure A)**.

3   Evenly distribute the cuff on the pant leg opening (it is wider than the cuff). To do so, stretch the fabric between two pins and place another pin **(Figure B)**. Continue stretching the fabric between pins and placing pins until the cuff is securely and evenly placed. Sew the cuff with a long, narrow zigzag stitch and trim the seam allowance **(Figure C)**.

4   Fold the leg cuff down and press **(Figure D)**.

5   Repeat steps 1–4 with the other pant leg.

A-Line dress

This versatile design offers a variety of options, from fancy to casual. The dress shown here is dolled up with a stretch lace overlay and bell sleeves. For a different look, you can use the pattern to sew a basic T-shirt dress made from a repurposed tee with straight sleeves and optional graphics on the front.

MATERIALS

Lightweight knit for main fabric, ¼ yard (0.2 m)

Stretch lace or coordinating fabric for overlay (optional), ¼ yard (0.2 m)

Thread: Coordinating with main fabric and the lace overlay fabric.

Sew On Soft & Flexible Velcro or Sew On Snag-Free Velcro (for lace fabric), 5" (12.5 cm) length

A-Line Dress pattern pieces: Front, Back, Sleeve, Large Ruffle (optional) or Small Ruffle (optional)

Note: This pattern shares pattern pieces with the Long Sleeve Tunic.

All seam allowances are ¼" (6 mm) unless otherwise noted.

FABRIC NOTES

Main fabric: Use a knit with at least a 2-way stretch across the grain, with a moderate stretch to a super-stretch percentage. This dress can be made with a variety of knits with good stretch recovery, from T-shirt fabric to a drapey knit. If you add ruffle sleeves, use a knit with great drape.

Overlay fabric: Use a stretch lace with at least a 2-way stretch across the grain, with a moderate to a super-stretch percentage and a good stretch recovery. For sheer sleeves, cut the sleeves out of lace only. To add to the drape on ruffled lace sleeves, use a no-fray stretch lace and leave the ruffle sleeve unhemmed.

UPCYCLE TIP

This is a great pattern to make from a repurposed T-shirt (see the striped dress at the end of this section).

1   Using the pattern pieces, cut out the fabric. Transfer the notches and dots on the pattern to the fabric with a disappearing-ink fabric marker (see Transferring Pattern Markings in chapter 1 for tips).

Refer to **Figure 1** *for steps 2–5.*

2   Sew a single-fold hem on each of the Front and Back pieces of the main fabric and lace overlay, if including one (see Sewing Hems in chapter 1 for directions).

Note: If you are not including a lace overlay, you can skip to step 4.

3   With right sides up, pin the lace overlay Front to the main fabric Front at the side seams, armholes, shoulders, and neckline (not the bottom edge). The lace overlay will overlap the main fabric by ¼" (6 mm) along the bottom edge. Sew the pinned edges together with a regular zigzag stitch on the edge using no seam allowance. In the same manner, pin and sew the Back lace overlay and Back main fabric pieces together.

4   With right sides together, pin the Back pieces to the Front piece at the shoulders. Sew the shoulder seams with a regular zigzag stitch and trim seam allowances.

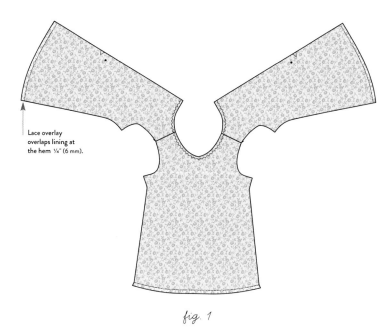

Lace overlay overlaps lining at the hem ¼" (6 mm).

fig. 1

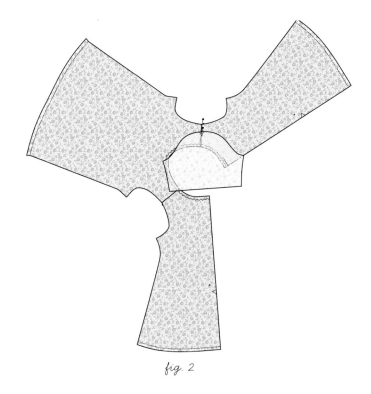

fig. 2

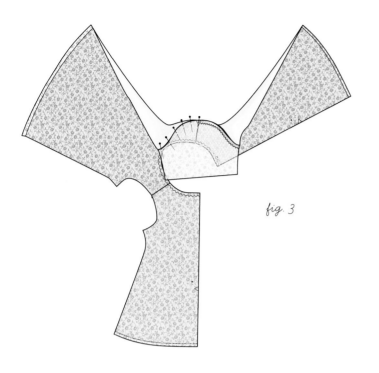

fig. 3

5   Following the Sewing Hems directions in chapter 1, finish the neckline with a single-fold hem using a long, narrow zigzag stitch.

6   With right sides together, match the notch on the sleeve with the shoulder seam at the top of the armhole and pin (**Figure 2**). Pin the edges of the sleeve cap to the edges of the armhole, then continue pinning the fabric between the end pins. Sew across the pinned portion of the sleeve with a regular zigzag stitch (**Figure 3**). Trim the seam allowance. Repeat this step with the other sleeve.

7 Finish the sleeve using one of the following options:

Straight sleeve: Sew a single-fold hem with a long, narrow zigzag stitch or a double needle for elbow, ¾-length, or long sleeves (see Sewing Hems in chapter 1).

Ruffle sleeve: Sew a single-fold hem on the outside curve of the large or small ruffle (not necessary for no-fray fabrics). Match the large ruffle with the elbow-length sleeve or the small ruffle with the ¾-length sleeve. With right sides together, line up the edge of the inner curve of the ruffle with the sleeve edge. Pin the curved edge to the straight edge, then use a regular zigzag stitch to join the two pieces together (**Figure 4**). Trim the seam allowance and fold the ruffle down to the right side. Repeat to sew a ruffle on the other sleeve.

8 Add a Velcro closure to the back (see Velcro Closures for Tunics and Dresses in chapter 1 for directions).

9 With right sides together, line up the front and back of the dress. Pin the pieces together from the sleeve edge, along the arm, and down the side seam. On the bottom hem, the lace overlay is ¼" (6 mm) longer than the main fabric.

10 Use a regular zigzag stitch along the arm and side seams. Trim the seam allowances and clip the underarm curve (**Figure 5**). Turn the dress right side out.

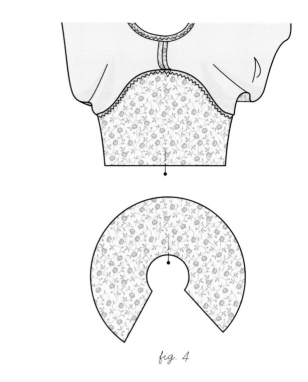

fig. 4

fig. 5

ABOVE: This casual version of the A-Line
Dress features three-quarter sleeves.

Long sleeve tunic

This stylish top has options for straight sleeves or bell-sleeve ruffles. It shares the same sleeve options as the A-Line Dress (see that pattern for more tips). If making the top with the lace overlay, cut the main fabric at the upper cut line (refer to the templates).

MATERIALS

Lightweight knit for the main fabric, ¼ yard (0.2 m)

Stretch lace or coordinating fabric for the overlay, ¼ yard (0.2 m)

Soft Velcro or Snag-Free Velcro (for lace fabric), 4" (10 cm) long

Thread: Coordinating with main fabric and the lace overlay fabric

Long Sleeve Tunic pattern pieces: Front, Back, Sleeve, Large Ruffle (optional), Small Ruffle (optional)

Note: This pattern shares pattern pieces with the A-Line Dress.

All seam allowances are ¼" (6 mm) unless otherwise noted.

FABRIC NOTES

Main fabric: Use a knit with at least a 2-way stretch across the grain, with a moderate to a super-stretch percentage and a good stretch recovery.

Overlay fabric: Use a stretch lace with at least a 2-way stretch across the grain, with a moderate stretch to a super-stretch percentage and a good stretch recovery. For sheer sleeves, cut the sleeves out of lace only. To add to the drape on ruffled lace sleeves, use a no-fray stretch lace and leave the ruffle sleeve unhemmed.

1   Using the pattern pieces, cut out the fabric. Transfer the notches and dots on the pattern to the fabric with a disappearing-ink fabric marker (see Transferring Pattern Markings in chapter 1 for tips).

*Refer to **Figure 1** for steps 2–6.*

2   Sew a single-fold hem using a long, narrow zigzag stitch or a double needle on each of the Front and Back pieces of the main fabric and lace overlay, if using one (see Sewing Hems in chapter 1). If you are using a no-fray fabric, you can leave the hem unfinished.

Note: If you are not including a lace overlay, you can skip steps 3 and 4.

3   With right sides up, pin the lace overlay Front to the main fabric Front along the side seams, armholes, shoulders, and neckline (not the bottom edge). The lace overlay will overlap the main fabric by ¼" (6 mm) along the bottom edge.

4   Using a regular zigzag stitch, sew the pinned edges together with no seam allowance. In the same manner, pin and sew the Back lace overlay pieces to the main fabric Back pieces along the side seams, armholes, shoulders, neckline, and the back opening.

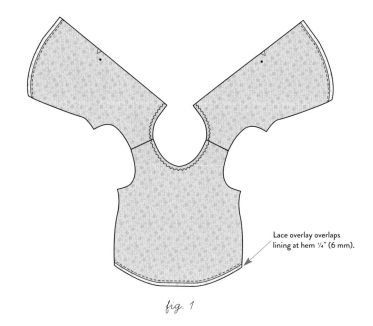

Lace overlay overlaps lining at hem ¼" (6 mm).

fig. 1

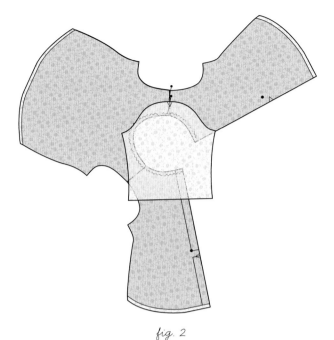

fig. 2

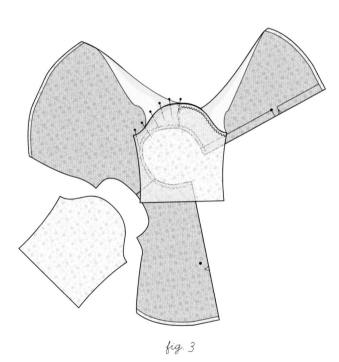

fig. 3

5   With right sides together, pin the Back pieces to the Front piece at the shoulders and sew with a regular zigzag stitch. Trim the seam allowance.

6   Following the directions in Sewing Hems in chapter 1, finish the neckline with a single-fold hem using the long, narrow zigzag stitch.

7   With right sides together, match the notch on the sleeve with the shoulder seam at the top of the corresponding armhole (**Figure 2**). Pin the edges of the sleeve cap to the edges of the armhole, then continue matching and pinning the sleeve cap to the armhole between the pins. Using a regular zigzag stitch, sew across the pinned portion of the sleeve (**Figure 3**). Trim the seam allowance. Repeat this step for the other sleeve.

8 Finish the sleeve using one of the following options:

Straight sleeve: Sew a single-fold hem with a long, narrow zigzag stitch or a double needle for elbow, ¾-length, or long sleeves (see Sewing Hems in chapter 1 for directions).

Ruffle sleeve: Add the large ruffle to the elbow-length sleeve or the small ruffle to the ¾-length sleeve. First sew a single-fold hem on the outside curve of the large or small ruffle (this is not necessary for no-fray fabrics). With right sides together, line up the edge of the inner curve of the ruffle with the sleeve edge. Pin the curved edge to the straight edge, then regular zigzag stitch the two pieces together (**Figure 4**). Trim the seam allowance and fold the ruffle down to the right side. Repeat for the ruffle on the other sleeve.

9 Add a Velcro closure to the back (see Velcro Closures for Tunics and Dresses in chapter 1 for directions).

10 With right sides together, pin the front and back pieces together from the sleeve edge, along the arm, and down the side seam. On the bottom hem, the lace overlay is ¼" (6 mm) longer than the main fabric.

11 Regular zigzag stitch along the arm and side seams. Trim the seam allowances and clip the underarm curve (**Figure 5**).

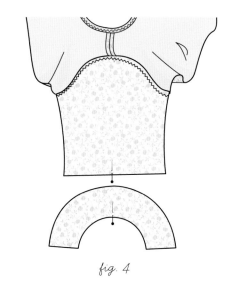

fig. 4

fig. 5

CIRCLE SCARF

MATERIALS

Light- to medium-weight knit with 4-way super stretch, ⅛ yard (11.5 cm)

Coordinating thread

¼" (6 mm) trim, 23" (58.5 cm) length

Pins

FABRIC NOTES

Main fabric: Use fabric with a lot of stretch and great stretch recovery. This will make it much easier to construct the scarf when having to turn it right side out.

This slim circle scarf can be doubled around a doll's neck without looking bulky.

1 Cut a 2" × 23" (5 cm × 58.5 cm) rectangle from the main fabric.

2 With right sides together, position the flat edge of the trim along one long edge of the fabric rectangle and secure with pins or wonder tape. Fold the fabric in half lengthwise with right sides together (the trim is now sandwiched between the layers). Pin or tape the long edge and sew with a straight stitch, starting and ending 2" (5 cm) before the edge of the fabric. Turn the scarf right side out.

3 Open the unstitched ends so they are flat and pin with right sides together. Sew with a straight stitch (**Figure 1**). Finger-press open.

4 Turn the stitched ends to the right side. Fold under the seam allowance ¼" (6 mm), pin, and topstitch the pinned section.

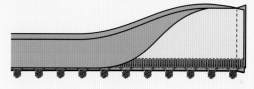

fig. 1

Leggings & Jeggings

These fashionable leggings look great with the Long Sleeve Tunic, Flutter Sleeve Tunic, or Athletic Top. For a cozy outfit, layer them under dresses or a skirt. Hem the leggings at the capri length included on the template for a summery look. You can sew them in a solid color, wild prints, or a knit that looks like denim for jeggings.

MATERIALS

Light- to medium-weight knit, ¼ yard (0.2 m)

Thread: Coordinating with main fabric and waistband

⅝" (1.5 cm) fold-over elastic, 10½" (26.5 cm) strip

Leggings and Jeggings pattern pieces: Front, Back, Waistband, Waistband Marking Guide

All seam allowances are ¼" (6 mm) unless otherwise noted.

FABRIC NOTES

Main fabric & Waistband: This pattern requires lots of stretch! Use a 4-way, super-stretch fabric with good stretch recovery (see Fabric Notes in chapter 1 for tip). Use the same fabric for the waistband. Be sure to match stripes and patterns when cutting the fabric. If you want the look of denim, use a stretchy knit that looks like jeans (stretch denim does not have enough stretch to work with this pattern).

UPCYCLE TIP

Instead of buying fabric, cut the pattern pieces from repurposed stretchy leggings.

1   Using the pattern pieces, cut out the fabric. Transfer the notches on the pattern to the fabric with a disappearing-ink fabric marker (see Transferring Pattern Markings in chapter 1 for tips). Cut at the capri line for ¾-length pants. Sew the capri leggings the same as the regular leggings.

2   With right sides together, pin a front and back leg together at the side seams. Sew with a regular zigzag stitch and trim the seam allowance (**Figure 1**). Repeat with the other leg.

3   Arrange the Front and Back pieces with right sides together, matching the double notches at the center back. Pin the center back and center front together, then sew with a regular zigzag stitch (**Figure 2**). Reinforce the seam. Clip the curve in the seam allowance.

4   Finish each leg with a single-fold hem using a regular zigzag stitch (**Figure 3**) or a double needle (see Sewing Hems in chapter 1 for directions). Press the seam.

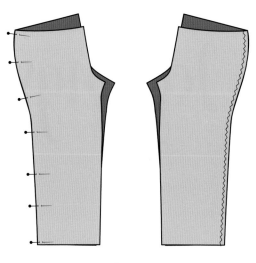

fig. 1

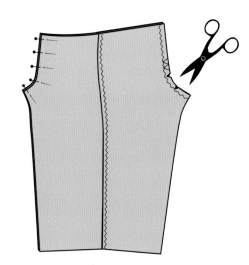

fig. 2

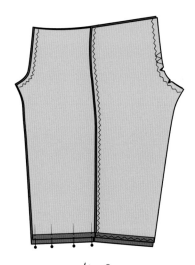

fig. 3

fig. 4

5 Referring to **Figure 4** and with right sides together, refold to match the center front to the center back. Pin the Front and Back pieces together at the center seams (to reduce bulk, pin seam allowances in opposite directions so they lie flat). Pin the front and back hem on each leg, then continue pinning along the entire inseam. Sew along the inseam with a regular zigzag stitch. Reinforce the seam. Clip the curve.

6 Turn the leggings right side out and press the inseam, center front and center back.

7 Add the waistband to finish the pants using a regular zigzag stitch on all the seams (see Adding a Knit Waistband in chapter 1).

Lace kimono cardigan

Featuring an attached kimono sleeve and a lace trim hemline, this stylish cardigan pairs well with pants, skirts, and dresses. Add length to the look and dress it up with dramatic 2" (5 cm) wide lace trim or use a small and subtle trim for a sweet touch. If you leave off the trim, finish the edge with a double-fold hem to match the cardigan front opening. Before cutting the back out of fabric, be sure to connect the right and left back pattern pieces.

MATERIALS

Light- to medium-weight knit, ¼ yard (0.2 m)

Thread: Coordinating with main fabric and waistband

¼-2" (6 mm–5 cm) lace or trim, 12⅞" (32.5 cm) strip (13⅜" [35 cm] if it frays)

Lace Kimono Cardigan pattern pieces: Front, Back 1, Back 2

All seam allowances are ¼" (6 mm) unless otherwise noted.

FABRIC NOTES

Main fabric: This pattern works with a variety of low- to super-stretch knits with at least a 2-way stretch across the grain. A natural drape will make the best kimono sleeve, so look for fabric with a good drape. I love making the Lace Kimono Cardigan out of a soft lace. Style it for summer with white lace and white lace trim. Use a patterned mesh or patterned lace for dramatic effect.

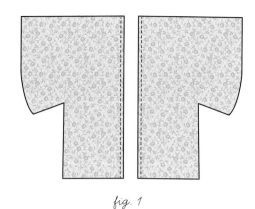

fig. 1

1   Using the pattern pieces,
    cut out the fabric. Transfer
    the notches and dots on the
    pattern to the fabric with a
    disappearing-ink fabric marker
    (see Transferring Pattern
    Markings in chapter 1 for tips).

2   Following the Double-Fold
    Hem directions in chapter 1,
    finish the long edge of the two
    Front pieces (**Figure 1**).

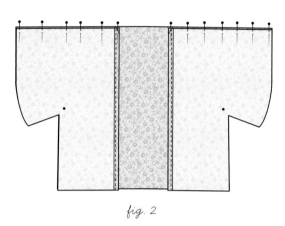

fig. 2

3   With right sides together, match
    the notches on the Front and
    Back pieces. Pin along the
    shoulder seam between the
    notches and the end of the
    sleeve (**Figure 2**).

4   Starting at one end of the
    shoulder, stitch across the
    shoulder seams. With wrong
    side out, press the shoulder
    seam allowance across the
    neckline toward the back.

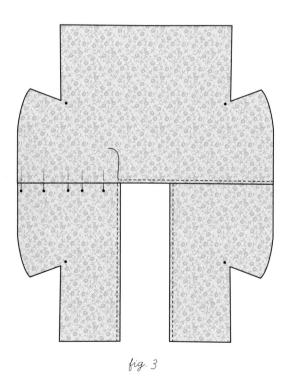

fig. 3

5   From the right side of the
    fabric, pin the seam allowance
    toward the back (**Figure 3**).
    Topstitch the seam allowance to
    the back and press.

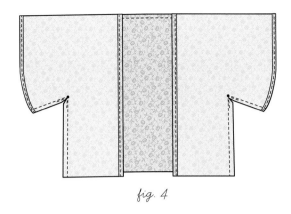

fig. 4

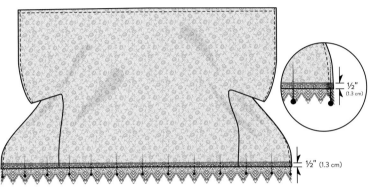

½"
(1.3 cm)

½" (1.3 cm)

fig. 5

6 Following the Single-Fold Hem directions in chapter 1, finish the sleeve edges.

7 With right sides together, pin along the side seams and sleeve seams. Sew the side seams from the bottom to the dot and then to the sleeve edges. Reinforce the corners. Clip into the corner on each side (**Figure 4**).

8 Turn the cardigan right side out. With the bottom edge flat, pin the trim to the fabric, overlapping the edge by ½" (1.3 cm) and sew (**Figure 5**).

Note: If the cut ends of the trim fray, first fold the ends of the trim ¼" (6 mm) to the wrong side of the opening before pinning.

Fur vest

This stylish fur vest is a hip addition to almost any outfit. Layer it with a dress or a cute top and leggings. You can make it out of a variety of faux-fur colors and textures for different looks.

MATERIALS

Fake fur, ¼ yard (0.2 m)

Lightweight knit for the lining, ¼ yard (0.2 m)

Large pin or safety pin

Thread: Coordinating with main fabric

Fur Vest pattern pieces: Front, Back

All seam allowances are ¼" (6 mm) unless otherwise noted.

FABRIC NOTES

Main fabric: Faux fur comes on different backings that vary from flexible to stiff. Choose a fabric with a flexible backing. Textured fleece is also an option. To cut out the fabric, arrange the pattern pieces on the backing.

Lining fabric: Use a lightweight knit because it makes the vest easier to turn right side out. Use anywhere from a moderate- to a super-tretch fabric with at least a 2-way stretch.

OPPOSITE: To make this sweet knit dress, follow the directions for the A-Line Dress using the three-quarter sleeves option.

1   Using the pattern pieces, cut out the fabric.

2   With right sides together, pin the lining Front pieces to the lining Back at the shoulder seams. Sew together with a regular zigzag stitch across the shoulder seams (**Figure 1**).

3   With right sides together, pin the fur vest Front pieces to the fur vest Back at the shoulder seams. Sew together with a straight stitch across the shoulder seams (**Figure 2**).

4   Lay the lining on the fur vest with right sides together. Pin the lining to the vest all the way around the edge except for the front and back side seams. Sew the pinned areas with a straight stitch, sewing the corners a second time to reinforce them. Cut off the tip in the seam allowance where the front opening meets the neckline (**Figure 3**). Clip the curve on the vest Front.

fig. 1

fig. 2

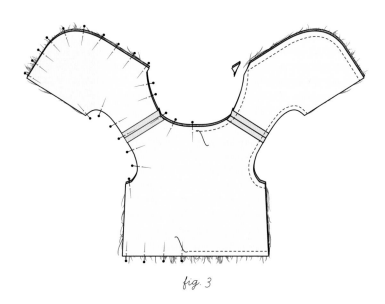

fig. 3

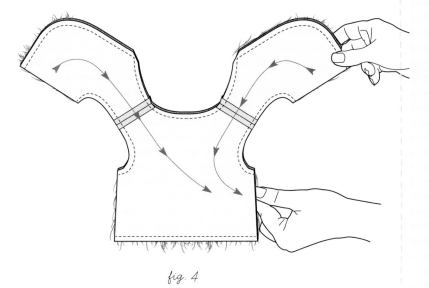

fig. 4

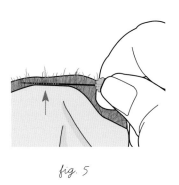

fig. 5

fig. 6

5 Referring to **Figure 4**, turn the vest right side out through the side seam in the vest back. Some of the fur ends will be in the seams of the vest. Slide a large pin or needle along the seam line to gently pull the fur, releasing the ends of the fur in the vest seams (**Figure 5**).

6 With right sides together, match the front and back side seams, pushing the fur out of the seam and pin along the side seams.

7 Straight stitch along the side seams, then regular zigzag stitch in the seam allowance to keep the edge clean (**Figure 6**).

8 Turn the vest right side out and gently pull the ends of the fur out of the side seams with a large pin or needle.

Glossary

Commonly used sewing terms that are used in patterns throughout this book are:

2-Way Stretch: Knit fabric that stretches perpendicular to the selvedge and has little to no stretch parallel to the selvedge.

4-Way Stretch: Knit fabric that stretches perpendicular and parallel to the selvedge.

Double-Fold Hem: A seam folded ¼" (6 mm) twice, with the raw edge enclosed.

Grain or Grainline: Direction of the fabric that is parallel to the selvedge edge.

Notch, Double Notch, and Dot: Markings on pattern pieces to match fabric, elastic, and trim.

Press: To iron fabric or seams.

Raw edge: The cut edge of the fabric.

Right Side: The side of the fabric that shows on a finished garment.

Selvedge: The prefinished edges of fabric yardage.

Stretch Direction: The direction a knit fabric has the most stretch. Typically it is perpendicular to the selvedge.

Stretch Percentage: Used to measure how much stretch a knit has when it is stretched perpendicular to the selvedge. (Use the stretch guide in the downloadable Templates PDF to measure stretch percentage.)

Topstitch: Stitching parallel to the seam or edge of the fabric on the right side of the fabric.

Wrong Side: The side of the fabric that's on the inside of a finished garment.

Acknowledgments

Christie Perkins challenged me to live bravely. While battling cancer, she encouraged me to not wait but stand up and live my dreams each day. She influenced where I am today, writing this book.

Thank you to Amelia Johanson, who suggested the idea for this book and walked me through the process to get me started. A huge thanks to Jodi Butler for coordinating and juggling the details. Thank you to Missy Shepler for her beautiful illustrations.

A huge thank you to all who have encouraged me and cheered me on: family, friends, and the online community at Doll-It-Up.com.

ABOUT THE AUTHOR

I am a lifelong maker and creator. I learned to sew watching my mother create beautiful things.

I was first drawn to doll fashion to connect with my daughter, creating outfits and scenes to build spaces for imagination and play. Today, combined with my passion to encourage creativity in others, I create projects and doll clothes patterns that are easy to follow and beautiful to make. I am the blogger, pattern designer, and teacher behind Doll-It-Up.com.

My current adventure is in southern Utah, where I've discovered the beauty of the desert: The bluest skies and vibrant hues of red and orange on the land. I am married to my husband of twenty years and have four children.

Metric Conversion Chart

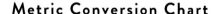

TO CONVERT	TO	MULTIPLY BY
Inches	Centimeters	2.54
Centimeters	Inches	0.4
Feet	Centimeters	30.5
Centimeters	Feet	0.03
Yards	Meters	0.9
Meters	Yards	1.1

INDEX

Keep Expanding Your Skills

WITH THESE OTHER GREAT TITLES

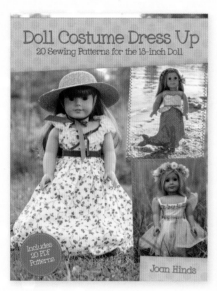

Doll Costume Dress Up

20 Sewing Patterns for
the 18-inch Doll

JOAN HINDS

978-1-63250-181-3

$25.99

Heritage Doll Clothes

Sew 20 American Outfits
for Your 18-Inch Dolls

JOAN HINDS

978-1-4402-4631-9
$24.99

See Kate Sew

24 Learn to Sew Projects You Can
Make in an Hour

KATE BLOCHER

978-1-4402-4545-9

$26.99